Children's Party Games

Children's Party Games

MICHAEL JOHNSTONE

WARD LOCK

A WARD LOCK BOOK

First published in the UK in 1994 by Ward Lock
Wellington House, 125 Strand, London WC2R 0BB

A Cassell Imprint

Reprinted 1995

Distributed in the United States
by Sterling Publishing Co., Inc.
387 Park Avenue South, New York, NY 10016-8810

Distributed in Australia
by Capricorn Link (Australia) Pty Ltd
2/13 Carrington Road, Castle Hill, NSW 2154

British Library Cataloguing-in-Publication Data
A catalogue record for this book is available from the British Library

ISBN 0-7063-7291-3

Typeset by MS Filmsetting Limited, Frome, Somerset

Printed and bound in Great Britain

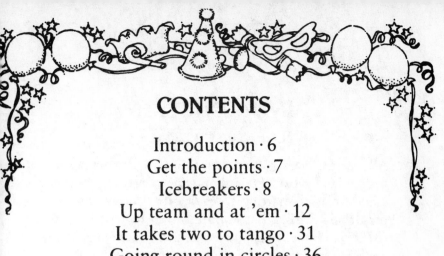

CONTENTS

Introduction · 6
Get the points · 7
Icebreakers · 8
Up team and at 'em · 12
It takes two to tango · 31
Going round in circles · 36
Follow my leader · 54
Blindfold fun · 55
It's mime time · 58
Paper and pencil games · 61
Musical madness · 69
A miscellany of games · 73
All the fun of the fair · 90
Seek and ye shall find · 92
Now is the time to say goodbye · 95
Forfeits · 96

INTRODUCTION

All parties need some preparation – children's parties more than most. Adults may be perfectly content to stand around chatting to each other, occasionally sipping their drinks, but children need to be entertained.

If your budget runs to it, you may consider hiring a conjurer to come in for an hour or so and baffle young audiences with astonishing tricks – rabbits that come out of hats, coins that disappear before the eyes, and cards that appear from nowhere. But most children enjoy parties where there is music to dance to and lots of games to play.

There are team games, games to play in pairs, musical games, observation games, paper and pencil games – all sorts of games. Some of the games that follow are best played outdoors: a few have to be played outdoors and are only suitable for summer garden parties. But most of the games in this book can be played indoors and at any kind of children's party – birthday, Christmas, fancy dress, barbecue or whatever.

With some pre-planning the situation described by Richmal Crompton in her book *William's Crowded Hours* can usually be avoided:

'As the fun of Ginger's party waxed fast and furious and one crowd of boys pursued another crowd of boys with ear-splitting whoops up the front stairs and down the back, Ginger's mother wrung her hands and said plaintively to William's mother: "if only ..."'

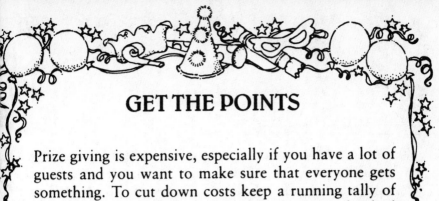

GET THE POINTS

Prize giving is expensive, especially if you have a lot of guests and you want to make sure that everyone gets something. To cut down costs keep a running tally of who won what. Give three points for an individual outright win; two for being a member of a winning team; and one for every game played and lost. At the end of the party give the two league leaders prizes – and encourage them to share them with everyone else.

If, however, you want to give the winner of each game a prize, have a bran tub. Wrap up all the prizes – and include a few spoof ones like empty boxes, tins of beans, etc. Winners select their own reward and take tub luck – anything from a comic to a lump of cheese.

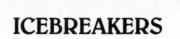

ICEBREAKERS

You know what it's like at the start of a party – especially children's parties, when everyone arrives within a minute or two of each other. Guests stand around feeling just a little awkward. Here are some 'icebreakers' that encourage everyone to get to know each other and get into the swing of things.

HAPPY FAMILIES

If you have a pack of 'Happy Families' cards, sort out one family for every four guests. Everyone draws a card on arrival and has to find the other three members of their family. As soon as they are *en famille* they sit on the floor and, while they're waiting for the others to get together in their fours, keep them occupied with ...

A DINOSAUR DRIVE

Each family is given a dice, four bits of paper and four pencils. Players take it in turn to throw the dice. They need a six to start, for that allows them to draw the dinosaur's body. The other parts are as follows:

> 5 for the head (one of these)
> 4 for the legs (four of them)
> 3 for the eyes (two of them)
> 2 for the horns (two of them)
> 1 for the tail (only one of them)

Players can fill in the legs and tail before they throw a five, but they can't fill in the eyes or horns on a headless dinosaur.

HUNT THE BALLS

Write the name of each guest on a ping-pong ball. As soon as the guests arrive, give each of them the ball with their name on it and send them off to hide them – anywhere they like within the party area. When the last to arrive has hidden his or her ball in some clever place, it's 'find the balls' time! The guest whose ball is last to be found is the winner.

AUTOGRAPH HUNTING

Give each guest on arrival a pencil and a sheet of paper with the names of everyone who's coming to the party printed neatly down the left-hand side. Everyone has to collect the autographs of everyone else. The last person to arrive feels like a film star as all the others mob her or him, clamouring for an autograph. There's no winner – but everyone soon gets to know who everyone else is.

A GOOD DOOK

'Dooking' for apples is a popular Hallowe'en game in Scotland, when the witches take to their broomsticks and fly through the air. It's a great icebreaker at any party. Float apples in a bucket of water and stand it just inside the party room on top of a towel or some sheets of newspaper. Before a guest is given a coke or orange squash he has to kneel in front of the bucket, hands behind his back, and bite an apple out. Thoughtful hosts and hostesses drape a towel around the shoulders of the 'dookers' before they plunge in.

FIND THE OTHER HALF

Cut up old colour supplement ads in two, horizontally, vertically, zig–zag – any way you want. On the back of one half, jot down a forfeit or a small prize (packet of jelly babies, tube of Smarties, etc.) and hide them around the house. Put the other halves in a hat. Arriving guests draw half an ad and are sent off to find the other bit. When they find it, they must perform the forfeit if they're unlucky enough to have drawn a forfeit card. Or they claim their prize – which is labelled with a forfeit...

MADISON AVENUE

Save old magazine and colour supplement ads for a couple of weeks before the party and either cut out or delete the name of the product. Pin them all over the house before guests arrive. As soon as everyone takes their coats off, give each of them a piece of paper and a pencil and send them away to list all the products in the ads. A quarter of an hour after the last guest has arrived, collect all the lists: whoever has identified most is the winner and he or she takes all – takes all the adverts off the walls, that is!

WHOSE PARENTS?

A favourite icebreaker at adult parties is for everyone to bring a snapshot of themselves taken when they were babies. These are hung round the room and a prize is given to whoever identifies most.

The following variation is great for children's parties: Put a note in with each invitation asking each guest to bring a photograph of either their father or mother, preferably taken when they were teenagers ... Did people *really* wear clothes and shoes like that? And just look at the hair!

CINDERELLA'S SLIPPERS

Get guests to take off both their shoes as soon as they arrive and when everyone is there put all the shoes in a pile in the middle of the floor. Boys rummage for a pair of girl's shoes and the girls look for a pair of boy's ones. Then, armed with a pair of shoes each, everyone rushes around like Prince Charming trying to find Cinderella – that is, the owner of the shoes they've taken from the pile. Last player to find the feet that fit gets a forfeit.

AM I PRINCE?

Pin the name of a well-known pop star on the back of each guest when they arrive and give them a pencil and piece of paper each. Tell everyone how many letters there are in their names and send them off to work out who they are. Players ask each other 'Is there an 'a' [or 'b' or 'c'] in my name?' The answers are either 'Yes' or 'No', and if there is more than one of the same letter in the names, the players have to work that out for themselves. Once they've written down the letters, they have to unscramble them and find out who they are. Now, who on earth is *yepathluccram*?

FARMYARD FUN

Make two or three teams – one team are the cows, another the sheep and the third (if you have one), the hens. Scatter lots of buttons all over the room. Tell everyone to get down on all-fours to root and peck around for the buttons, making the appropriate animal noises as they go. When a player picks up a button he takes it to the hostess, who keeps score, and goes off to look for another one. The team that collects the most buttons wins.

BALLOONING AROUND

Give everyone a balloon as soon as they arrive. Make sure that there's an even number of balloons of the same colour and distribute the colours evenly between boys and girls. When everyone has arrived and blown up their balloons they have to pair off with someone with the same colour, put the balloons between their knees and keep them there as they dance together. Couples leave the floor if either balloon floats from its moorings. The winners are the last couple left on the floor.

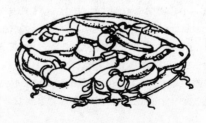

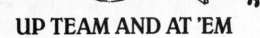

UP TEAM AND AT 'EM

'The team spirit is all very well for those for whom that sort of thing is all very well', is Miss Jean Brodie's damning assessment of team games. But most children love them, so here is a selection of some of the most popular team games and races.

For team relay races, the first team back in its original position is the winner.

The simplest way to form teams is to stand everyone in a circle and number them. For two teams, the even numbers make up one team and the odd numbers the other. For three teams, numbers 1, 4, 7, 10 form the first team, 2, 5, 8, 11 the second, and 3, 6, 9, 12 the third. And so on.

Another way of forming teams is to put an assortment of coloured bands, cards, buttons, tiddlywinks or anything small into a bag and let everyone draw something out of it. Be sure that there's an object for each guest and the same number of matching-coloured objects in the bag.

Right! Get into teams and off we go.

MATCHLESS FUN

Give each team a matchbox cover. The first player slips it on to the end of his nose. On the word 'Go!' he transfers it on to the next person's nose, without using his hands, and so it goes, nose-to-nose, down to the end of the line. When the matchbox cover is securely on the last player's nose, he or she runs to the front of the line, and so the race progresses until the original front man is back at the head of the line. Use of the hands is cheating and, when the game is over, any player guilty of this should be given some dire forfeit (see page 96). If the box drops off someone's nose, it goes back to the front again.

SPOON BALL

Line up teams of players giving them all a spoon which they hold between their teeth. Team leaders are given a ping-pong ball which they put in the spoon. They have to pass it on to the next person, who passes it to the next – and so on down the line – without using their hands. If the ball is dropped it goes back to the leader and starts its trip all over again. When it reaches the last player in the teams, they run up to the front of the line, ball in spoon, spoon in mouth, and start off all over again.

THE HERRING RACE

The 'herrings' are teaspoons, securely tied to the free ends of cotton reels. The herrings are placed at one end of the room. The cotton is unwound and the reels given to the first in each team, who are standing on chairs. They bring the fish in by spinning the reels between their fingers – overhand winding is not allowed. When they have landed their herrings, they throw them back to their original positions (best have an umpire to put them back against the wall), give the fishing lines to the next players and run to the end of their teams.

THE BALLOON RACE

Line up teams at one end of the room and give the person at the front of each team a balloon, which has to be held between the knees. 'Ready! Steady! Go!', and the leaders race to the other end of the room and back again. If any balloon floats to the floor, whoever let it go must return to base and start again. The balloon is given to the next player in turn . . . Best have some reserve balloons blown up, just in case!

WHO'S FOR THE HIGH JUMP?

Make sure all breakables are out of the way! Line up teams at one end of the room and hang a line about half a metre (20in) from the floor between them and the far end

of the room (a rope tied between two chairs is ideal).
Give each team leader a ball, and when the starting
signal is given they have to run up to the rope, jump over
it, touch the wall at the far end of the room and throw
the ball to the next in line. When everyone has jumped
the hurdle, the last player gives the ball to whoever was
first in his team and the game continues until the teams
are back where they started.

EGG AND SPOON RACE

Everyone is given a spoon as in 'Spoon Ball' (see page
13), but this time leaders are given an egg as well. With
spoons in mouths, the egg is passed from player to
player, spoon to spoon – no hands allowed. When it's
safely in the last man's spoon, he runs with it to the front
of the team. And it goes down the line again – and again,
and again – until the team is back as it started.

HANG THE WASHING

Stretch a clothesline across one end of the room and put
a basket of old clothes in front of it, containing one
garment per player and enough clothes pegs to hang
them up. On the 'off' the first player in each team runs to
the clothes basket, grabs a garment along with a couple
of clothes pegs and hangs it on the line. Then he dashes
back to his team and the second player runs up to hang
out something . . . When a team has all its washing on the
line, it starts to rain! So one by one the team members
make for the line and remove whatever they hung up.
First to get the washing in wins.

HARE AND HOUNDS – STILL-LIFE VERSION

One team are the 'hounds', who are given two minutes
to tag as many 'hares' as possible. When a hare is caught
it must stand completely still. After two minutes
the hares become the hounds and the hounds hares.
Whichever team turns most hares into statues wins.

THE CRAB RACE

Have you ever seen a crab scurry across the beach: sideways, backwards – but rarely forwards? Line up teams at one end of the room. On 'Go!' the first player gets down on hands and knees and crawls sideways to the far end of the room and back. The next to go has to crawl backwards for his run – then it's sideways for the third player, backwards for the fourth, and so on to the end of the line.

GETTING THE SACK

Old-fashioned, jute sacks are ideal for sack races, but heavy-duty black plastic ones do just as well. The first to run in each team pulls the sack up to his waist and tries to get his feet into the corners before heading for the finishing line and back to give the sack to the next in line. Hopping is cheating.

BLOW MAN BLOW

Put a ping-pong ball on the floor in front of each team and give everyone a straw. On 'Go!' the first player gets down on hands and knees and blows the ball through the straw to and from the far end of the room – then the next, and the next – until everyone is quite out of puff.

WAITER! WAITER!

Form teams of eight players and give the head waiter – the man at the front of each team – a plate with three ping-pong balls on it. On 'Go!' he runs down the team and back to the front again, weaving in and out of the others in line as he goes. He has to hold the plate as if he was a waiter – balanced on his upturned hand. Naturally, if the balls roll off the plate he has to go back and start again. The second player has to run round the front man before heading down the line and back to his original place. And the third weaves his up, down and up before giving the plate to the fourth ...

POTTED BALLOONS

Ever tried balancing a balloon on an empty yoghurt pot and keeping it there as you run to the back of your team? It's far more difficult than it looks, but that's what you have to do in this race. The leader runs round the team and gives the pot and balloon to the second in line, who runs round the leader, down to the end of the team and back to his place before giving the potted balloon to Number 3 ... If anybody drops the balloon off the pot the team has to start all over again.

BATTLESHIPS

Each team is given as many squared sheets of paper as there are teams. There are 400 squares, numbered one to twenty along the top and 'A' to 'T' down the side. On one sheet each team outlines its own fleet, and on the others it charts the attacks made on enemy fleets.

Fleets are marked as follows:
   One aircraft carrier (five squares adjoining
      either horizontally or vertically)
   Two frigates (four squares each)
   Three submarines (three square each)
   Four minesweepers (two squares each)
   Five cruisers (any five random squares)

Teams take it in turn to attack the others' fleets. They call out the squares – A1, C9 or whatever. If they score a hit, they get another turn. If they miss, another team gets a chance to fire its guns. The winning team is the one with any part of its fleet intact – even a fifth of an aircraft carrier – when everyone else's has been sunk.

BLOW FOOTBALL

You need a table, a ping-pong ball and two teams for this. Seat the teams on either side of the table and put the ball in the middle. When the whistle blows, teams try to score by blowing the ball over their opponents' edge of the table. You can play in several ways:

1 The player who lets the ball through is sent off and the game goes on until all the players in one side are in the 'cooler'.
2 Play for five minutes: whichever team scores most goals wins.

If there are more than enough players for two teams, form as many teams as you want and play a knock-out competition, with the winners of the early rounds going on to the semi-finals and finals, just like the FA Cup. Or you can play on a league basis with everyone playing everyone else – three points for a win, two for a score draw, one for a no-score draw, nothing for a defeat.

UP JENKINS!

Keep the same teams as you had for 'Blow Football' and the same table. One side is given a coin that they pass under the table, player to player. At any time, someone in the opposite team can call out 'Up Jenkins!', and the side holding the coin at that moment has to raise clenched fists into the air. On the command 'Smashems' they bring their fists on to the table top and open them up so that their palms are downwards on the table. Next, when 'Creepie Crawlies!' is shouted, hands are pulled towards the edge of the table. Whenever anyone in the opposing team thinks he knows where the coin is, he leans across the table and taps the hand under which he thinks it lurks. If he's right, the coin is given to the opposition. If he's wrong, whichever side had the coin put their hands under the table and pass the penny to each other until someone cries 'Up Jenkins!' again.

TEAPOT

One team goes out of the room and the other decides on a word – for example, 'sleep'. When the first team comes back each member takes it in turn to ask his counterpart on the opposing side a question to help him guess the word. The word 'teapot' must be used in every question.

'Do we all teapot?'
'Yes.'
'Do we teapot outside or inside?'
'You can do it wherever you want.'
'Do animals teapot?'
'Yes.'
'Do we teapot in the kitchen?'
'You could, but it's not the usual place.'
'Do we teapot in bed?'
'Most of us do.'
'It's "sleep".'

... and the other side go out to allow time for a new 'teapot' to be chosen.

SUCKERS

Put a pile of tissues at the far end of the room, opposite each team. Give everyone a straw. The first man runs to the tissues, sucks one on to the end of his straw and keeps it there while he runs back to transfer it to the next player, who has to suck it off with his straw. The second player runs to the end of the room, blows his tissue onto the floor and sucks up another ... the best suckers win the race.

CLAPPER

Sit couples down in a long line facing each other – about a metre (3 ft) between each pair. The 'Clapper' stands between the two lines armed with a supply of ping-pong balls. There are two fielders behind each line. When the 'Clapper' shouts 'Go!' the pair at the end of the lines run up the backs of their teams trying to dodge the balls thrown by the 'Clapper' and the fielders. The winning team is the one whose players make it to the top with the least number of strikes against them.

THE GRAND NATIONAL

Teams stand in line, each player bending over, his arms tightly around the waist of the person in front, forming one long horse. The player at the rear of each team jumps on to the back of the player in front and straddles his way to the front. If he falls off or lets his feet touch the ground, he has to go back to the starting-post again. When he's safely at the front of the horse, he leapfrogs over its shoulders, everyone steps back a place and the new jockey at the back is under orders and 'off'.

ELBOW TO MOUTH

Give each team leader a tennis ball. Once they have it securely between their elbows, they pass it to the next in line who bites at it until the ball is gripped firmly between his or her teeth. It then goes to the next player's elbows, then on to the following mouth, until it reaches the end of the line. Then, the man at the end of the line runs to the front, with the ball either between his elbows or in his mouth, and down it goes again, elbows to mouth. If a player drops the ball, he throws it back to the front man.

THE ORANGE ANKLE GAME

Two teams sit facing each other with their legs stretched out in front of them. The host balances an orange on the ankles of the team leaders. Somehow they have to pass them to the next-in-lines' ankles. They try to get it nestling on the third pair of ankles ... If an orange rolls to the floor, it goes back to the leader again. The first team which successfully passes the orange, ankle to ankle, from first player to last, wins.

DRESS THE SCARECROW

Stand one player from each team at the far end of the room beside a pile of old clothes. He or she is the scarecrow and stands like Worzel Gummage, quite limp, giving no help at all to the players, who take it in turn to run up to him and dress him in the old clothes. Make sure there's one article of clothing for each team member in their pile. Have an old jacket, trousers, pair of Wellies, a shirt, scarf and a hat. First team to dress Worzel wins.

SHOE THE HORSE

The 'horses' are chairs stabled at the far end of the room opposite the teams, each one cared for by a 'groom'. The 'shoes', four washing-powder cups, should be on the seat. The first from each team runs up to the horse and 'shoes' it by putting one cup under each leg of the chair. When the horse is properly shod, the blacksmith runs back to his team to tag the next to go. Meanwhile, the groom removes the shoes and puts them back on the seat. It may sound easy, but before the blacksmiths set to work, the groom blindfolds them – and the blindfolds are only removed when the horse's shoes are properly in position!

THREAD THE SNAKE

Give each team a teaspoon tied to a very long piece of string. The first player threads the spoon up through his clothes and gives it to the next in line, who threads it downwards from jumper neck to trouser bottom. And so the 'snake' weaves its way up and down the team, until the last player in each team is holding it aloft. Now the winning team is blindfolded and everyone else watches as they try to unravel themselves.

THE BOTTLE RACE

The first person in each team is given a plastic lemonade bottle. On 'Go!' they put it between their knees, then try to get it between the knees of the next in line. When (or if!) it gets to the last player, he waddles up to the front of the line and everyone moves down a place and the bottle race starts again.

IT'S A KNOCK OUT

You have, repeat, *have* to play this in the garden, unless you happen to live in an enormous house and have a gallery or two to spare. Lay out an obstacle course before the party. Form two teams. On the order 'Go!' the first player in each team makes his way round the course, through rubber tyres, under groundsheets, over the high jump . . . When he or she is back to base, the second starts his circuit. Or, when the first obstacle has been cleared the next to go can start. Here are a few ideas for obstacles:

1 Hang tyres from convenient branches, one per team. Players have to manoeuvre themselves through them.
2 Put down sacks for a sack-racing run.
3 Mark out a long jump.
4 Make a high jump. Players clear it before going on.
5 Have a short (very short!) water jump.
6 Mark out part of the course that must be hopped across by runners – wearing Wellington boots.
7 Lay skipping ropes on the ground. Players can't go for the next obstacle until they've completed ten consecutive skips.
8 An egg-and-spoon dash. If a player drops the egg, he starts again.
9 Stretch tarpaulins across part of the course. Players have to crawl under them.
10 The last part of the course has to be somersaulted over.

You'll need stewards at each obstacle to ensure that each one is properly cleared before runners attempt the next, and to take Wellies, sacks, eggs and spoons back to starting points.

SIAMESE TWINS

The first and second players in each team hold hands and face each other. The host puts a tennis ball between their foreheads. They have to keep it there as they run to the far end of the room and back. If the ball drops, they have to go back and start again. When the first couple have successfully completed their run, the ball is put between the second pair's foreheads, and then the third, and so on.

AND THE BAND PLAYED

Form teams of four or five players and give each one the following equipment:

> eight empty milk bottles
> a jug of water
> spoons
> rubber bands
> a ruler
> a comb
> tissue paper

The teams have five minutes to create their own musical instruments, five minutes to rehearse and then they entertain the other teams, who vote for the best band. Teams can't vote for themselves.

Rubber bands stretched around the ruler will produce various notes when plucked if the bands are tightly stretched to different tensions.

To make a xylophone, fill the bottles to different levels. Each one produces a different note when struck by a spoon.

Wrap the paper round the comb to make a mouth-organ.

Spoons tapped together sound like castanets.

SLAP HAPPY

Players sit side-by-side, legs akimbo. There should be a chair at either end of each team. On the front chairs are ten coins. As soon as the starting signal is given, the player at the front picks up one of the coins and puts it in the upturned palm of his left hand. He passes it to the next in line, by slapping it on their upturned right palm. The coin is slapped left-hand palm to right-hand palm down the line to the last man, who puts it on the chair beside him. As soon as the first coin is safely on the third-in-line's palm, the player at the front starts the second coin on its journey down the line. The winning team is the one that's first to have all ten coins on the back chair.

NOUGHTS AND CROSSES

Use masking tape to mark out a large noughts and crosses grid on the floor. One of the teams is the noughts and the other is the crosses. Toss a coin to decide which team goes first. Both teams try to position three of their players in three adjacent squares, while trying to prevent their opponents from doing the same. Players who are on the board when the other side succeeds in lining up three of their players leave the game, which goes on until one team doesn't have enough players to continue playing.

SNAKES AND LADDERS

Make two teams and sit them down facing each other, about half a metre (20 in) between each pair, with their legs outstretched so that their feet are touching the opposite player's. Number each pair. When a number is called, that couple hop over the outstretched legs down to the end of their teams' lines, race up the back and hop down to their starting positions. First to sit down gains a point for his team.

HAS-BEANS

The team leaders hold a plate containing ten baked beans and one cocktail stick for everyone in their team. So, if there are six players in each side, there will be sixty beans and six sticks on the plates. When the starting signal is given, the leader spears his ten beans into his mouth, one by one. When he's swallowed them all, he passes the plate to the next in line, and so it goes on. Incidentally, in 1981 Karen Stevenson took just thirty minutes to eat 2,780 beans with a cocktail stick: that's just over one-and-a-half per second! Ask the teams to try and beat that!

VOLLEY BALLOON

Form two teams and stand them either side of some string stretched across the middle of the room at about shoulder height. Stand the teams in square formations – a line of players at the 'net', a line at the back, and one line at either side. Teams score by landing a balloon on the floor of their opponent's court. They can pass the balloon four times before making a shot, but if someone drops a balloon on his or her side, it's a point against them. Players must stay rooted to the spot they are in until, when the balloon touches the floor, everyone moves one place clockwise: this gives everyone a chance to be at the net and make scoring shots.

THE COACH PARTY

Before the party the hostess makes up a story about a family outing that brings in Mum, Dad, Peter, Pat, Garfield the cat, Rover the dog. If it's a really big party, she can include Granny, Grandpa, Old Uncle Tom Cobleigh and all ... there has to be a role for every person in a team. The teams sit in circles and the hostess starts to read. Whenever a character's name is mentioned, that person in each team stands up, cries 'That's me!', spins round three times and sits down again, earning a point for his or her team in the process. When the word 'family' is mentioned, everyone stands up, shouts 'That's us!' and spins round. If a player or family haven't started by the time the first on their feet have shouted, spun round and taken their seat, they lose a point. Get someone to keep score.

THE TRIVIAL PURSUIT GAME

Form four teams. You should have coloured bands for each team or some other means of identification, as teams become muddled up as the game progresses. Teams throw a dice to decide the playing order. The question-master stands in the middle of the room armed with a supply of questions. Teams start off in their own corner.

The question-master asks the captain of the first team a question. If the captain gives the right answer, he moves on to the next corner, and the question-master asks the second player in the first team a question. If that's answered correctly, both he or she and the captain move on a corner. When a wrong answer is given, the question-master turns the spotlight onto the next team. The first team to have all their members back to base wins.

CRACKERS

Each player is given a cream cracker. On 'Go!' the leaders cram their crackers into their mouths and swallow them as quickly as possible. As soon as their mouths are empty (and you can test this by making players whistle), the second in each team starts to crumble their crackers into their mouths. First team to eat all their crackers wins. Their prize is to be first in the queue for a glass of water.

BOAT RACES

Get teams in line and give everyone a plastic beaker of water. Arm the team leaders with a towel to drape over their shoulders. On 'Go', the team leader drains the beaker as quickly as possible, turns it upside down on his head and passes the towel to the next in line. Only when the first beaker is empty and in position can the second player start drinking. The first team to have everyone with a beaker on his head wins.

FRUITY FUN

Two teams of equal numbers stand against opposite walls. Each team member is given the name of a fruit – so there's an apple, an orange, a banana, a lemon, a pear, etc., in both teams. One player is the fruit seller. He or she shouts out the name of a fruit. That fruit in each team changes places, while the fruit seller tries to beat one of them to a vacant place. Whoever's left out is the next fruit seller. If you have enough guests you can play with four teams, one team standing against each wall.

UP AND UNDER

This is another game for the garden! Leave about half a metre (20 in) between each team member and a metre (1 yd) between the lines of teams. The man at the back leapfrogs over the man in front, dives between the legs of the next player, leapfrogs the third, and so on. As soon as a player has been jumped over or crawled under, he moves back a place. As soon as the first to go has reached the front of the line, the new man at the back takes off. The first team back in their original positions wins.

FIREMEN

Put a bucket of water in front of each team and a saucepan at the back. The leaders are given a cup which they fill from the bucket and pass down the team. When it gets to the last man, he empties it into the saucepan, sends it back up the line again and the race continues until the first team has filled the saucepan. It may be wise to play this game in the garden, too.

GIANT'S FOOTSTEPS

The first person in each team is given two sheets of paper – both just big enough to stand on. They have to go from one end of the room to the other and back again, putting one foot on the first sheet of paper, then placing the other sheet a step in front and standing on that in turn. Now they have to balance on one foot, turn, bend down to pick up the first sheet and put it down in front of the second ... and so on. Anyone whose foot touches the carpet has to start again. The sheets are passed to the next one in line and the fastest team with the fewest faults wins.

BALLOON BALL

Two teams sit opposite each other, legs stretched out in front with feet touching. Right-handed players put their right hands behind their backs. Left-handed players put their left hands behind their backs. The referee throws a balloon between the teams. Whoever manages to catch it tries to score by throwing it over the heads of the other team. The team with most goals wins.

PANCAKE RACES

The 'pancakes' are sheets of newspaper cut into 30 cm (12 in) squares and put in two piles at the far end of the room, opposite both teams. The 'frying pans' are pairs of garden canes cut down to an appropriate size. Give the pans to the first players in each team. On the command 'Ready! Steady! Go!', the cooks run up to the pancakes, somehow manoeuvre one into the frying pan and run to the back of their team. They put the pancakes on the floor, then pass the frying pan up the line to the new man at the front who races for the pancakes ...

THE GREAT WELLIE RACE

All the players have to do in this simple team relay race is, when it's their turn, help the player in front take off the pair of Wellies that were at the other end of the room, put them on, run to the far wall and back to the next person. It would be easy if the Wellies weren't several sizes too large for the contestants ... It's even more fun to give each team only *one* Wellie – and make it a hopping race.

THE WALL GAME

One end of the garden is the finishing line, which players in one team try to touch before they are 'tagged' by players in the other. The attackers stand in a circle, arms linked, going round and round. The defenders stand between them and the finishing line. At any time he or she wants, the leader of the attackers can shout 'Go!' The circle breaks up and the players in it dash to the finishing line. If a player is tagged he stands where he is. Now the defenders become the attackers. Whichever team gets most players to base wins. This game must be played outdoors.

SHOOT!

Two teams line up with their backs to each other, about half a metre (20 in) apart. Players stand open-legged, their feet touching those of the players on either side, and bend over so that they are looking at the other team from between their legs. Toss a coin to decide which team has first possession of the ball. On 'Go!' the teams try to score goals by throwing the ball between the legs of a player on the opposing team. Players can pass the ball amongst themselves before a shot is attempted. Play this game outdoors, and *don't use a hard ball*.

STEP BY STEP

In this team relay-race, players have to get to the far end of the room and back, walking heel-to-toe, and 'tag' the next in line. Anyone losing his or her balance has to go back to the start again.

ROLL THE LEMON

Team leaders are given a lemon and a pencil each. On 'Go!' they push the lemon to the end of the room and back using only the point of the pencil. When they get back to their teams, they give the lemons and pencils to the next to go and run to the back of their teams . . .

THE DERBY

The 'horses', one for each team, are pieces of paper folded in two lengthways and balanced on a piece of string each. One end of the string is tied round a chair and the other end is given to the leader. They have to manipulate their horses to the chairs without letting them fall off the strings and without using their free hands. If a horse falls, its jockey has to take it back to the starting line and begin again. When a horse gets to its chair, its jockey takes it off the string, runs back to the next to go and gives him the horse for his ride ...

FALLING LEAVES

You need a pack of cards and a waste-paper basket for each team. On 'Go!' the captain runs to the basket, picks up the cards, and holds the first one with the long edge against the top of his nose before letting it fall, hopefully into the basket. When the host shouts out 'Change!' (after fifteen seconds), the players at the basket pick up the cards scattered on the floor, run back to their teams and give the next player all the remaining cards. The first team to get the entire pack into their baskets is the winner. Easy? Try it.

THE BEER MAT RACE

Teams of six players sit in lines and the leader has six beer mats in front of him. On the starting signal the player at the top of each line picks up the first beer mat, holding it between the tips of his forefingers – left on top, right underneath. He gives it to the next player, removing his finger from the top once that player has got his left finger in position. When the second player has the beer mat firmly between his two forefingers, he turns it upside down and passes it to the next player ... As soon as the mat is with the third player, the leader starts to pass the second mat, then the third ... The winning team is the one whose last player is first to collect all six mats.

THE THIMBLE AND STRAW RACE

Teams stand in lines. Each player is given a straw which he holds in his mouth. Team leaders are given a thimble each. On 'Go!' the thimble is passed down the teams, straw to straw, with no hands allowed. When it's safely on the last straw, the player runs to the head of the team, still with the straw in his mouth and the thimble on the straw, and the next round begins.

CLIPPED AND UNCLIPPED

Two teams sit in line, facing each other, and everyone is given a paperclip to hold behind their backs. 'One! Two! Three! Start!' The first player passes his clip to the second, who attaches it to his clip before passing them to the third. When the last man has the complete clip-chain he holds it between his knuckles and puts it on the lap of the player next to him. He has to pick it up, also with his knuckles, and pass it onto the next player's lap . . . and so on down the line. As soon as the chain has reached the front man, he puts it behind his back, removes one clip and gives the chain to the next player. When the last player has the last clip, he holds it aloft. First team with all their clips on display wins.

MUMMY! MUMMY!

One 'Mummy' stands facing each team holding a roll of lavatory paper. On 'Go!' the first in each team runs up to her, grabs the paper and starts to bandage her, beginning at the feet and working upwards. After fifteen seconds, the second player in each team dashes to the Mummy, takes the paper and continues to wind it round and round. If the paper tears, it must be tucked neatly into the folds before starting again. The first team to use all the paper wins. Don't forget to release the Mummy.

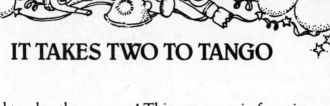

IT TAKES TWO TO TANGO

... and to play these games! This pot-pourri of pastimes for pairs contains races, chases and putting people through their paces.

It's best not to let children choose their own partners, for there may be one or two guests whom no one knows and who may feel left out. But there are lots of ways to pair everyone off. Have a bundle of cards for the girls and one for the boys. On the girls' cards you may have written the names of famous women with their partners' names appearing on the boys' cards. So, for example, the 'Queen' has to find 'Prince Philip'. Or you could have female animals on one set of cards and their male counterparts on the other. When everyone draws a card they have to make the appropriate animal noise to attract their partners. Cows *moo!* sheep *bah!* pigs *oink!* ...

GETTING HOOKED

Send all the girls out of the room and give each boy a pencil tied to a long piece of cotton. One by one the boys throw their lines over the door and girls queue up to take turns at catching the 'bait'. Anglers are paired off with their catches and the games can start.

SOMERSAULT RACES

Somersault races are fun as long as your guests do not mind a few bumps and bruises. Divide all the children into pairs and get one of each to lie on his back, feet on the starting line. Partners stand over them, facing the line, and bend over to grab their partners' ankles. At the same time the players on the ground take hold of their partners' ankles. And they're ready! With that they're off, somersaulting over and over towards the finishing line.

BUSY BEES

There has to be one odd man out for 'Busy Bees'. He stands facing all the couples and orders them to 'Hold each other's hands!'; 'Stand shoulder to shoulder!'; 'Sit back to back!', or anything that comes to mind. Whatever he says has to be obeyed, but when he calls 'Busy Bees' everyone has to change partners and the caller tries to get one for himself. Whoever is left on his or her own when the others have new partners shouts the orders for the next round.

WHEELBARROW RACES

These are best run in the garden, but are just as much fun in a large room. One of each couple gets down on hands and knees behind the starting line. Their partners pick them up at the knees so that their feet are sticking out at either side! Ready! Steady! Go! (If you can!) The first pair to make it to the finishing line wins.

THREE-LEGGED RACES

If anyone has enough energy left, stand each couple side-by-side behind the starting line with their inside legs tied together. The first to cross the finishing line deserves a prize for good balance.

WELL I'LL BE BLOWED!

Give each pair a balloon. Tell one of each couple to blow it up and tie it securely by the neck. Now the fun starts. The second player in each pair tries to blow up a balloon while being beaten about the head with the other one. It's amazingly difficult to blow when being attacked in this way! Whichever couple succeeds first in holding up two blown-up balloons wins. Now untie all the balloons and let the air out. The attackers in the first round become defenders in the second, for it's the turn of those who were being hit with the inflated balloon to get their revenge.

PAPER FASHIONS

Put a pile of newspapers and rolls of Sellotape on a table. One of each couple has to make an outfit for his or her partner to wear. Give them fifteen minutes before holding a fashion parade with everyone voting for what they think is the best and most imaginative paper suit. Not their own, of course.

SPILL THE BEANS

Give everyone the same number of beans, and each couple a mirror and an empty yoghurt pot. One of each pair of partners holds up a mirror. The other puts the pot on his head and tries to drop the beans into it, one by one. When all the beans are in the pot – or on the floor – the players change round and the one who was holding the mirror gets a chance to spill the beans. The couple with most beans in the pot are the winners. You can also play this game with jugs of water!

HANG ON!

Because your opponent is going to try to pull you off your stool! (If there are younger children playing this, stand an adult behind each stool to catch them as they tumble.) Stand the players on top of a low stool each about three metres (10 ft) apart. Give them a piece of rope, five metres (17 ft) long. 'On 'Go!', both of them reel in the loose rope until it's stretched tightly between them, and one well-timed yank will dislodge one of the contestants.

CATCH THE TRAIN

One of each couple stands behind his or her partner holding them at the waist. One player doesn't have a partner! On the starting signal, the linked couples – the 'trains', 'engine' at the front, 'carriage' at the back – run around the room while the player on his own – a loose carriage – tries to link into a train by grabbing hold of a carriage by the waist. If he succeeds, the engine is unhooked, the old carriage becomes an engine and the now uncoupled player tries to get himself hooked on to another train ...

PUSH-UPS

Make sure that everyone is paired off with someone roughly their own size. Stand them facing each other, right-hand palms pressed against the left-hand palm of the opponent. Now everyone takes one step backwards so that they are leaning heavily against each other's hands. No one is allowed to move their feet now, as each player pushes like mad, trying to make the other lose balance and topple over. Winners challenge each other to try out their strength. The outright victor is usually the pushiest person in the room!

NOAH'S ARK

Give everyone, except the guest playing Noah, a piece of paper with the name of an animal on it. There should be two of each beast in the game – two donkeys, two cows, two cockerels, two snakes, etc. Now the lights are put out. All the animals are in the Ark and they've broken out of their pens: they're on all-fours braying, mooing, crowing, hissing ... Noah comes into the gloom to tell them that land has been spotted. He's got two minutes to pair off the animals by listening to the noises they are making.

ROLL THE BALLOON

Pairs stand facing each other, a balloon squashed between them at waist level. On 'Go!' everyone has to turn around three times – keeping the balloon between them. If it falls to the floor or bursts in the frantic attempts to keep it in place, the couple responsible leaves the game. In the next round everyone turns around four times, then five, then six – and so on, until there are only two couples left spinning round and round and one of them lets go or bursts the balloon. The couple with the last balloon still intact are the winners.

THE JOLLY MILLER

The Jolly Miller leads couples around the room, everyone singing the following little ditty:

> There was a jolly miller who lived by himself.
> With lots of corn he made his wealth.
> One hand was in the hopper,
> The other in the bag.
> As the wheel ground on, he fell off the shelf.

On the word 'shelf' everyone has to find a new partner, and the miller tries to find himself a wife (or husband), by grabbing a free player. Whoever is left on their own takes over the mill.

BRAVE SIR FRANCIS

This is best played outdoors and although girls can play it, the game is a favourite with boys. It's rough-and-tumble time! One of each pair gives his partner a piggy-back. The 'knight', who is armed with a pillow or cushion, uses it to try to knock other 'knights' off their horses. Brave Sir Francis can be either the last knight remaining on his horse after a general free-for-all, or the winner of a knock-out tournament!

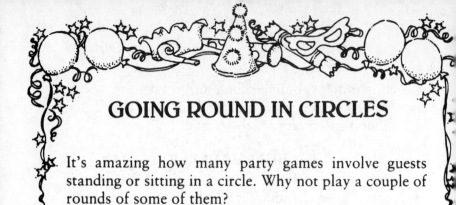

GOING ROUND IN CIRCLES

It's amazing how many party games involve guests standing or sitting in a circle. Why not play a couple of rounds of some of them?

RUSH HOUR

The player standing in the middle of a circle of seated players has to get himself a seat. He does this by ordering players to change places – 'Players with black shoes change seats with those wearing ribbons in their hair,' or, 'people with blonde hair swap seats with brunettes.' In the mad rush that follows, the traffic controller tries to grab himself a chair, and whoever is left standing at the end of one rush hour tries to seat himself next round.

BEAUTY AND THE BEAST

Choose and blindfold the 'Beast'. Now select 'Beauty' without letting the Beast know who she is. He stands in the middle of the circle and Beauty tiptoes into it, as far away from him as possible. When the Beast calls out 'Where are you Beauty?' she must reply, 'Here, Oh Beast!', and then tiptoe away before the poor beast can catch her. When he does get her in his grasp, he has to guess who she is before taking off his blindfold. If he's right, another Beauty and another Beast are chosen. If he's wrong, he has to try again with a different Beauty.

A B C D F G H

The first player recites the alphabet but leaves out one letter. The second player – the one next in the circle – goes through the alphabet again, leaving out the same letter and then omitting one of his own. Anyone who includes a letter that was previously left out is out of the game, and the next player starts at the beginning again.

SPIN THE PLATE

Put a tin plate in the middle of the circle and number all the players. On the word 'Go!' the first player, Number 1, runs up to the plate and spins it on its edge. When it's whizzing round and round he calls out another number. That person has to get to the plate before it stops spinning, spin it again and call out another number. If he fails he loses a life. Three lives lost and you're out.

CATCH THE KLEENEX

The man in the middle holds a paper tissue above his head and, as he calls out the number of any of the players in the circle, he drops it. Whoever is called has to run into the middle and catch the tissue before it lands on the floor. If they're too late, they lose a life. You can play this game with balloons, in which case it's called 'Catch the Balloon'.

HEADNICKS AND PINTICKS

Give everyone three *spent* matches. Players hold one of them on the floor under their right-hand forefingers, making sure that no one can see if the head is pointing towards their finger-nail or away from it. The first to go has to guess which way the match under the player on his right's finger is pointing. If he thinks the head is nearer the nail, he calls 'Headnicks': otherwise he call out 'Pinticks'. A correct guess gains the caller the hidden match, a wrong one costs him one of his own. When a player runs out of matches he leaves the game.

SPOOF...

...is great fun for older children. Sit the players around a table. They should all have three coins hidden in their left hands. When someone calls out 'Spoof' they put none, one, two or all their coins into their right hands, cover them with their fists and bang them on the table. Now players take it in turn to guess the *total* number of coins in the fists. (Best get an adult to note all the guesses, thus avoiding any squabbling.) If there are ten players, there could be as many as thirty coins hidden (if everyone had three in their fists), or none at all. When the fists are opened, whoever was farthest out leaves the table.

SOFT TOUCH

This game, also known as 'Hand in Hand', was once banned in England. The story goes that it was so popular at the royal court that no one did any work! So the king made it illegal! Happily a later monarch, we don't know which, changed the law, and now we can all enjoy it again. Everyone stands in a circle, except one player who tiptoes round the outside. When he touches one of the others on the back, they chase him round and round the circle. The chaser can take short cuts across the circle but the 'toucher' can't. When he's caught, he joins the players in the circle and his captor becomes the toucher.

THE ZOO GAME

The first player calls out the name of an animal that begins with the letter 'a'. Once he's called it out, he starts to count from two onwards. Before he's counted to ten, the second player has to come up with another animal that starts with 'a'. And so on round the circle. If anyone fails to come up with an 'a'nimal before the previous player has reached ten, he's out. When it's the next turn of the first player, he calls out an animal starting with 'b'.

COIN TO CARD

Players are given a card each. One of them has a penny balanced on it. Whoever holds that card has to pass the coin onto the next player's card without using his free hand. The coin goes around the circle, card to card. Anyone dropping it is disqualified. The game goes on until there are only two players passing the coin on to each other's cards, and one of them drops it.

JEREMIAH

The first player says, 'Jeremiah's coming to stay: I'll scratch my head.' And scratch he does until the second to go says, 'Jeremiah's coming to stay. I'll clap my hands.' Both players now scratch and clap at the same time until the third player tells the others that when Jeremiah comes to stay he'll jump up and down. The three scratch, clap and jump in unison – and so it goes round and round the circle, each player taking it in turn to announce Jeremiah's arrival and adding a new movement to the sequence! Anyone who loses the rhythm leaves the circle, leaving the others to their scratching, clapping, jumping, turning, nose wrinkling – whatever!

TIPTOES

'He' (or 'it') sits blindfolded in the middle of the circle of seated players and points to one of them. He or she must stand up without making any noise and start to tiptoe around the inside of the circle. When 'he' calls out 'Stop Tiptoes!', he must be obeyed. 'Tiptoes' stands still and 'he' tries to point directly at her. If 'he' manages this, Tiptoes leaves the game and 'he' points to another player to take her place. If 'he' misses, he and Tiptoes change places. The seated players have to remain quiet, but that doesn't mean they can't pull faces, trying to make Tiptoes give his or her position away by giggling.

THE FOOLISH DONKEY

The host says he's going to go around the circle whispering the name of an animal into players' ears. Then he tells everyone that when he gives the starting signal they should each make the noise of their particular animals. However, what he really says to everyone is 'Don't make a sound', except to one poor player to whom he whispers 'Donkey!'

'Go!' – and everyone has a good laugh as the donkey makes an ass of himself!

THE FRAGILE TOWER

Everyone is given twenty matches each. A bottle is placed in the middle of the circle. Players take it in turns to balance a match across the mouth of the bottle, and when the mouth is completely covered, they start building another layer, then another, and another . . . If one or more of the matches falls off, whoever is to blame adds them to his pile. The first player to get rid of all his or her matches wins. It's quite in order for a player to balance a match in such a way that the next to go is bound to knock some off!

NOW FOR THE GOOD NEWS

This game is based on the old joke about the surgeon who says to one of his patients, 'I'm afraid I've got some bad news for you: I'm going to have to amputate both your legs. But cheer up. There's good news as well.'

'What's that?', asks the shattered patient.

'The man in the next bed wants to buy your slippers!'

The first player starts the game by saying 'I've got some bad news for you all . . .', and goes on to tell everyone what it is. The second player then cheers the party up with some good news connected in some way to the bad news. Now the third brings the gloom down again with another piece of bad news. . .

Here's an example:

Player 1: 'I've got some bad news. The ship is sinking.'

Player 2: 'Yes! But there are places in the lifeboats for us all.'

Player 3 'Sadly, there are leaks in them!'

Player 4: 'That's alright. There's enough time for the ship's carpenter to fix them all.'

Player 5: 'He's drunk!'

Player 6: 'Er . . . em . . . Can't think of anything!'

PLAYER 6 IS OUT!

CHANGING SIDES

A caller stands outside the circle and numbers all the players alternatively '1' and '2'. As soon as everyone is numbered, they get down on all-fours. When the caller shouts '1s' they start to crawl forward, but they can only move one limb on each call, either an arm or a leg. When the caller shouts '2s' all the other players do the same. The aim of the game is to change places with the person opposite in the circle. It sounds easy, but half-way through there's an enormous traffic jam, with everyone crawling over each other's shoulders, between their legs – all over the place!

CATCH THE CANE

Number all the players in the circle and give one of them a walking stick. He stands in the middle holding the stick upright, one end on the ground, the other beneath the palm of his hand. When he shouts out a number, he lets the cane go. Whoever has been called has to get to the stick before it crashes to the floor. He then calls out another number. Players lose one life each time they don't make it to the stick in time. Three lives lost and they're out.

GIVING 'EM STICK

One player is blindfolded and armed with a walking stick. He then stands in the middle of a circle of players. The others walk round and round until the blind man manages to touch someone lightly with the stick. Now everyone has to stand still while the blind man makes an animal noise – he might baa like a sheep, or crow like a cockerel, for example. Whoever is touched makes the same noise to give the blind man a chance to guess who it is. If he's right, the two change places; but if he's wrong the circle moves round and round until he touches another player with the stick and succeeds in identifying him or her.

BEANS AND TOAST

The first player is given a book and begins to read from it, substituting 'beans' for words beginning with 'b' and 'toast' for words starting with 't'. When he makes a mistake, the book is passed to the next player.

Here's the first paragraph from *The Borrowers* – or perhaps I should say *Toast Beans*.

> It was Mrs Mary who first toast me about toast. No, not me. How could it have been me – a wild, untidy, self-willed little girl who stared with angry eyes and was said to crunch her toast. Yes, toast was it – Kate. Not toast toast name matters much either way: She beans come into toast story.

FLIP FLOP

The player in the middle says 'Flip!' and points to someone in the circle who must reply 'Flop!' Or, if the man in the middle says 'Flop!' the response should be 'Flip!' If he says 'Flip! Flop!' the answer should be 'Flop! Flip!' As the game goes on the 'flipping' and 'flopping' gets faster and faster, as more flips and flops are added. He who hesitates is lost, for if there's a delay of more than five seconds whoever was due to reply is OUT!

FOLLOW MY LEADER

One player stands in the middle of a circle of seated players. He tells the others that he is a train, or a motor bike, or any other kind of transport he wants to be, and runs around the circle making the appropriate noises and actions. When he touches someone's knee, that person has to get up and run behind the train, doing whatever he is doing. The leader taps another player, then another, until there's a line of players behind him. When he shouts 'Change!' everyone rushes for an empty seat. Whoever is left standing goes into the middle for the next round.

HOT POTATO

It doesn't have to be a potato. It can be a ball, small box, orange – or anything small that can be easily passed round the circle when the music is playing. But when it stops, whoever is left holding the 'hot potato' is out. The game goes on until there are two players left, frantically throwing the potato to each other, desperate not to have it in their hands when the music stops for the last time.

PASS THE PARCEL

Wrap a bar of chocolate in layer after layer of newspaper. When the music stops whoever is holding the parcel unwraps one layer. If the person hasn't finished unwrapping when the music restarts, he drops out, but if he has he passes the parcel on to the next player. So, it's music, pass the parcel, stop the music, unwrap, music, pass the parcel . . . Whoever unwraps the last layer keeps the chocolate, which should of course be shared with everyone else.

To make sure that there is more than one winner, you could put a small prize in each layer. Whoever successfully unwraps a layer is rewarded with a prize. Alternatively, you could put a forfeit in each layer. Whoever is holding the parcel when the music stops has to do whatever he's told to. (See page 96.) Another idea is to have a mixture of prizes and forfeits, so that no one knows if they're going to get a bar of chocolate or if they have to make an idiot of themselves in some way!

THE OK CORRAL

One player stands inside the circle. He's the 'wild steer'. The players in the circle are cowboys and girls who taunt the steer by putting arms or legs over the border line. If the steer succeeds in tagging a cowboy when part of his body is in the circle, the one who is touched becomes the steed, and the steed joins the cowboys. Brave cowboys make wild dashes right across the corral!

EVERYONE'S A FRUIT AND NUT CASE

In the middle of the circle put a huge bar of chocolate on a chair along with a tin plate, a knife and fork, a hat and a scarf. Players take it in turn to throw a dice. The first to get a six runs to the chair, puts on the hat and scarf and tries to eat the chocolate, using the knife to cut off a piece and the fork to get it into his mouth. Next to throw a six runs to the chair, helps the player already there to take off the hat and scarf and puts them on before starting to carve and fork the chocolate. The game goes on until the last crumb of chocolate has been eaten. If you don't mind the mess, you can play this game with a large bowl of Spaghetti Bolognese and a pair of chopsticks!

WINKIE

Set up a circle of chairs. Sit a girl on each chair except one. Stand a boy on guard behind every chair, including the vacant one. The boy behind the empty seat has to attract a girl to it by winking at her so discreetly that her protector doesn't notice the flicker of his eyelids. If the protector sees the wink and manages to get a hand on his partner's shoulder before she attempts to leave her seat, she must stay where she is. The 'winker' tries again until he's successful. Whoever is left behind the empty chair takes over as winker.

CHINESE WHISPERS

Whisper a message into the ear of the next person in the circle. He then whispers it to his neighbour, and so on around the circle until the message reaches the person on the other side of the one who began the whisper. He calls out what has just been whispered to him – it usually bears little resemblance to the original. Adults may remember hearing the story of the World War I message 'Send reinforcements: we're going to advance', which was eventually received as 'Send three-and-fourpence: we're going to a dance.'

GARFIELD THE CAT

The first player calls out 'Garfield the cat is an ...', and here adds an adjective beginning with 'a', followed by the word cat. (For example, 'an *angry* cat'.) The second player says, 'Garfield the cat is an angry...', and then adds an adjective starting with 'b', before finishing the sentence. And so on around the circle, players taking it in turn to remember all the previous descriptions before adding one of their own. And when someone calls the cat an awful, black, cheeky, dead, exceptional, flighty, generous, hard, intelligent, jaundiced, kinky, lazy, mad, naughty, opulent, pretty, quaint, religious, strong, tough, unwanted, violent, Welsh, xenophobic, zany cat ... the next person has to remember all that before starting over again with another 'a'! A player who takes too long or who makes a mistake drops out. The winner is the arrogant, bigheaded, conceited, disdainful ... player with the best memory!

ROUND THE WORLD

A blindfolded player stands in the middle of a circle of guests who take it in turn to call out the name of a country. The blind man listens carefully, and when he shouts out two countries, the players who called them out in the first place tiptoe across the circle to change places. The blind man has to try to get into one of the vacant chairs before it is reoccupied. Whoever is left stranded in the middle is the blind traveller next time round.

JUST A MINUTE

The host points to someone in the circle and calls out a letter. The player pointed to has sixty seconds to call out as many words as he can starting with the given letter, before pointing to another player in the circle and calling out another letter. The host keeps the score.

BUZZ

Someone calls out 'one'. The person next to him 'two', and so on round the circle. But at 'seven', any multiple of seven, or any number that contains a seven, the player must call out 'Buzz' instead. The order then reverses, so that whoever called out 'six' takes up the count again with 'eight'. It's easy until you get to 66 – that's when the problems really start. You'll see what I mean when you get that far!

SNAP HAPPY

Everyone in the circle is given a number. Or, if your guests are very quick-witted, two or even three numbers. Now! Altogether ... slap your hands on your thighs, *Slap!* Clap your hands, *Clap!* Snap the fingers of the left hand, *Snap!* And the fingers of the right hand, *Snap!* Got the rhythm? *Slap! Clap! Snap! Snap! Slap! Clap! Snap! Snap!* ... Once everyone's in the swing of it the host calls out a number on the second Snap! So it's Slap! Clap! Snap! *Six!* Number Six goes Slap! Clap! Snap', and then another number. If anyone loses the rhythm, or forgets to call out, they leave the game. Quicken the pace as the game progresses. 'Snap Happy' sounds simple, but just you try it!

THE MAN IN THE MIDDLE

The man in the middle of the circle taps his nose and points to someone else. This player has to tap his or her nose and then do something else – stamp a foot, say. The man in the middle taps his nose, stamps his foot and scratches his ear before pointing to another player, who repeats all three actions and then maybe spins round. Should the man in the middle miss out one of the sequence, the person who was last to go takes his place. If he has a good memory and looks as if he could go on forever, put a time limit of two minutes on each round. This way everyone gets a chance to be in the middle.

GOING PLACES

The 'tour guide' stands in the middle of the circle and points to the first player. He tells him or her where they're going and asks the 'tourist' to name three things to take on the journey, each one of which must start with the initial letter of the destination. If the tourist manages to do this within five seconds, he changes places with the man in the middle and chooses another destination and another player to call out three items. However, if he fails, he leaves the circle.

So, the game might go something like this:

'We're going to Aberdeen. What are we taking
with us?'
'Apples, ants and apes!'
'We're going to Paris. What are we taking
with us?'
'Pears, plums and plants.'
'We're going to Zaire! What are we taking
with us?'

Not so easy!

LAS VEGAS

The famous gambling capital of the world gives its name to this game. Players take it in turn to throw a pair of dice. Whoever throws the highest number goes first and may throw as often as he wants, adding whatever he threw in the preliminary round to his score. But, if a 'one' is thrown, his score is wiped out. The dice is passed to the second player who throws as often as he wants, again adding his score to what he threw in the preliminary round, and again, a 'one' cancels out his total score. The dice goes round and round the circle. On the second round, a 'two' cancels the score *in that round*. In the third round, a 'three' is the killer, a 'four' in the fourth, a 'five' in the next and a 'six' in the next. First to reach 100 wins.

THE RAT-CATCHER

The 'rat' is an old tin can filled with dried peas and sealed to make a rat-tle. The rat-catcher is blindfolded and stands in the middle of the circle. The person holding the rat throws it across the circle. Whoever catches it holds it for five seconds before throwing it to someone else. If the rat-catcher points directly at the player holding the rattling rat, he or she has been caught rat-handed and becomes the catcher.

CONNECTIONS

One player in the circle shouts out any word that comes to mind. The player on the right immediately calls out a word which has some connection with the first word. Players can challenge each other to explain the association. If there's no satisfactory explanation forthcoming, the one who called out the word leaves the game.

FIRST TO LAST

The first player calls out the name of a town and the player next to him shouts out another that starts with the last letter of the first. And so the game goes round and round the circle, players who can't think of a suitable town within ten seconds dropping out. 'Edinburgh! Hull! Liverpool! Leeds! Sunderland! Dundee! Evesham! Manchester! Rugby! York!' – this game will certainly improve your geography!

SPIN THE KNIFE

The man in the middle spins a knife and calls out any letter of the alphabet apart from 'X', 'Y' or 'Z'. Whoever is 'stabbed' (i.e. is opposite the point of the knife when it stops spinning), has sixty seconds to shout out as many words as he can think of starting with that letter. The player with the longest list wins. Change the knife-spinner every five goes so that everyone has a chance to show off their expertise.

CATCH A FALLING BALLOON

Give everyone in the circle a number. The player with the highest number is 'It' and goes into the middle for the first round. Holding a balloon, he spins round three times and calls out a number, dropping the balloon to the floor as he shouts. The player whose number is called has to run to the middle of the circle and catch the balloon before it touches the floor. If he succeeds he takes over as 'It'. If he's too late he loses a life, and the man in the middle spins again, drops the balloon and shouts another number.

CONSEQUENCES

An evergreen favourite. Everyone is given a strip of paper and a pencil and asked to write down a girl's name followed by the word 'met'. The paper is then folded over and passed to the next person in the circle and everyone writes down a boy's name followed by the word 'at'. Another fold before it goes on for a meeting place – the funnier the better. Fold again, pass and write 'He said. . .' Fold, pass and write 'She said. . .' Fold once more pass and write 'And the consequence was. . .' Fold for the last time and pass. And now each one in turn reads out their 'story'. The results can be hilarious – whether you use famous people or the names of friends.

SIMPLE SIMON AND THE PIEMAN

'Simon' and the 'Pieman' stand in the middle of the circle. The others are the pies, and they sit holding hands. 'Simon, the pies are on fire,' shouts the Pieman. They both run to someone in the circle and try to pull him or her into the middle. If they succeed, the pie becomes one of the Pieman's assistants and helps Simon and the Pieman pull a pie from the oven next time they burn. If, however, the pies can pull Simon, the Pieman or one of his assistants out of the circle, *they* burn and one of the pies is promoted to Pieman.

I, THE MAD MAHARAJAH...

...chants the player in the middle of the circle, pointing to someone in it. 'I do not like the letter "s". What will you give me to eat?' The player being pointed to must suggest something that does not contain that letter. Cake would be quite acceptable, but biscuits would be poison to the Mad Maharajah. So would swedes, but turnip would be all right. The Mad Maharajah points to someone else and announces the next poison letter. Anything suggested must contain neither the first nor the new poison letter. Change the man in the middle after every five goes. Anyone who accidentally poisons the Maharajah is out of the game.

NAME DROPPING

The player in the middle of the circle throws a ball to anyone he chooses, at the same time calling out a letter of the alphabet. The catcher has five seconds to shout out a first name that starts with that letter before throwing the ball back to the man in the middle. Players who either drop the ball or cannot think of a name in time leave the game. If the man in the middle calls out a difficult letter such as 'Q' or 'Z', the catcher can challenge him to come up with a suitable name if he can't think of one himself. If the challenge is successful and the man in the middle is unable to think of a name within five seconds, the two change places.

ANIMAL ADJECTIVES

Everyone in the circle has a number. Number 1 calls out an animal that starts with 'a' and an adjective to describe it, also starting with 'a'. He then calls out another number and he or she continues the game with 'b'. For example, the game might start with: 'The angry ape! Number 8!' Player 8 could then call out 'The busy bee! Number 10!' And Player 10 continues with 'The cool cat!...'

CAT AND DOG

This is a very simple game which causes gales of laughter. One of the players is given two small objects. He passes the first to the person on his right and says, 'Here's the dog!'

'The what?', he or she asks.

'The dog!', repeats the first player. And so the dog is passed around the circle, everyone repeating 'Here's the dog!'

'The what?'

'The dog!'

When the second player is passing the dog to the third, the first player hands the second object to the player on the left.

'Here's the cat!' he says.

'The what?', asks the player on the left.

'The cat!', says the first player...

The fun starts when the dog and the cat cross. It becomes difficult to remember what animal you have in your hand. Anyone getting the two confused leaves the circle. The faster the dog and the cat are on the move, the more difficult the game becomes.

GET KNOTTED

On 'Go!' everyone closes their eyes, runs into the centre of the circle and grabs the first two hands they come across. Now they open their eyes and try to untangle themselves without letting go of the hands they are holding. Players get into all sorts of difficulties as they climb over and under each other, between legs, over shoulders – all over the place!

CHICAGO

Another dice game named after an American city. Players throw two dice. They only score if they come up with a specific number for each round. Anything else doesn't count. In the first round players have to throw two 'ones'. They score two points. Nothing else counts. In the second round, they must throw a 'two' and a 'one' to score three. For the third round they must throw four (either two 'twos' or a 'three' and a 'one'). And so it goes, until the eleventh round when only two 'sixes' count. Appoint an umpire to keep score.

CAPITAL CATCH

The man in the middle of the circle throws a ball to one of the players. As he throws he calls out the name of a country. Whoever catches the ball has five seconds to come up with the country's capital before throwing the ball back to the middle. A player who doesn't know the answer leaves the game, but before he does so, the man in the middle has to prove that he knows the capital of the country he called.

DOMINOES

Players in the circle stand sideways as close as possible to the person in front. On 'Go!' everyone tries to sit down very slowly so that eventually all the players are seated on the knees of the people behind. Naturally if anyone tumbles backwards, the whole circle collapses like a domino-snake and everyone ends up on the floor. But if, by some miracle, they make it right down, tell them to try to scurry round!

THE CIRCLE LINE

Seat players in a circle of chairs, leaving a reasonable space between each one. The caller stands in the middle. When he shouts out an odd number, players must move that number of places to the left, sitting down briefly on every chair they pass. If an even number is called, they go to the right. As soon as he has called the number, the man in the middle forces his way into the circle ... Whoever is left unseated at the end of a round goes into the middle.

PASS THE RING

Thread a ring on a piece of string long enough to go right around the circle of players. The man in the middle tries to follow its progress as it passes from hand to hand along the string. Players confuse him by pretending to pass the ring when they don't have it. When the man in the middle thinks he knows who is holding it, he cries 'Stop!' and points to who he thinks it is. If he's right, they change places. If he's wrong the game continues.

MUSICAL SPOONS

Players kneel, their hands behind their backs, in a small, tight circle around a cluster of spoons. There is one less spoon than there are players. When the music stops everyone tries to grab a spoon, but as there's one less spoon than there are players, someone is bound to be left empty handed. He or she is out. The spoons are replaced in the centre of the circle. One of them is removed and the music is restarted. The game continues until there are two players and one spoon up for grabs.

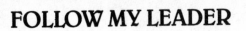

FOLLOW MY LEADER

These games involve having a leader. Choose him or her by getting all the guests to draw a card – the highest wins. Otherwise, stand everyone in a circle and spin a knife. Whoever it's pointing to when it stops is the leader.

O'GRADY

The leader, O'Grady, stands facing everybody else, who must do exactly as he does so long as he prefixes his orders with 'O'Grady'. So, if he says, 'O'Grady says put your arms in front of you,' and stretches his arms out, players must do just that. But if he commands 'Scratch your head,' and does it, no one else should. Anyone who does is out. The last person in becomes O'Grady for the next round. Start off slowly and then gradually speed up.

BANDMASTER

The guests pretend they're members of a band, with the leader as their conductor. A well-known tune is chosen for everyone to hum and the conductor accompanies his band on an imaginary instrument – piano, flute, trombone, whatever takes his fancy. The band must imitate his actions: so, if the conductor is scraping a make-believe violin, the band fiddle the air along with him. The conductor can change his instrument at any time – and the last bandsman to copy him leaves the bandstand. The last player in is conductor for the next session.

EAR! EAR!

In this game, players must do as the leader says, not as he does! If, for example, he shouts 'Chin! Chin! and points to his chin, players point to their own. But if he says 'Ear! Ear!' and points to his nose, anyone who points to his nose is out...

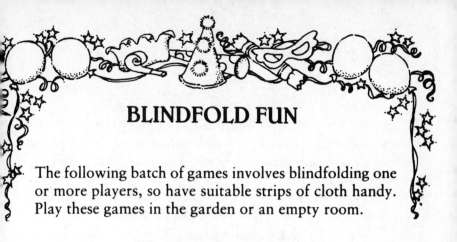

BLINDFOLD FUN

The following batch of games involves blindfolding one or more players, so have suitable strips of cloth handy. Play these games in the garden or an empty room.

HOBSON'S CHOICE

Blindfolded 'Hobson' stands beside a dressing-up trunk or bundle of old clothes in the middle of a circle of other players. They take it in turn to throw a dice while Hobson rummages amongst the clothes and holds up whatever he picks out. When a player throws a six he dashes into the middle of the circle, grabs whatever Hobson is holding aloft, puts it on and runs back to his place. Hobson selects another garment for the next to come up with a six – and the next, and the next. There's no winner, just a lot of fun and lots of giggles. The game goes on until Hobson has emptied the wardrobe.

RING THE BELL

In this game *everyone* is blindfolded, apart from one player who is given a bell. Don't worry if you don't have a bell, anything that makes a noise will do – even some dried peas in a glass jar. The blindfolded players fumble around the room trying to grab hold of the bell-ringer. Whenever anyone calls out 'Ring the Bell,' whoever has it is honour-bound to do so, thus giving the others a clue to his whereabouts. When a blind man traps the ringer, the two change places and the game goes on.

THE CHIMPS' TEA PARTY

Get everyone to find a partner and give each couple a bowl of cornflakes and two spoons. On 'Ready! Steady! Go!' everyone tries to spoon 'flakes into their partners' mouths. Whichever pair empties the bowl first are the winners. It's easy when you've got your eyes open, but much more difficult blindfolded! Do make sure that no one jabs the spoon at his or her partner: they have to move the spoon very slowly when finding their partner's mouth.

THE KEY TO THE DOOR

A boy and a girl are blindfolded. They get down on all-fours in the middle of the circle. The others hold two or three coins in their hands. On 'Go!' a set of keys is thrown into the circle and at the same time everyone starts to jangle their coins. The blindfolded players try to hear where the keys land and crawl towards them, hoping to be first to find them. Whoever get the keys removes his blindfold and changes places with someone in the circle, swapping the blindfold for the coins. The loser plays the newly-blindfolded player in the next round.

THE DONKEY'S TAIL

Draw a large, tail-less donkey on a sheet of paper or an old sheet and pin it to the wall. Make a tail, as long as you want, and either stick a drawing pin through the top or attach a piece of Bluetack on the inside, again at the top. Players take it in turn to be spun around three times and then set off, tail in hand, to fix it in the proper position. Very few manage to do this.

BLIND MAN'S BUFF

This was played hundreds of years ago by Queen Elizabeth and her courtiers – and was probably popular centuries before that. It still is. The blindfolded player is spun around three times and sent off to capture the others who, of course, do their best to avoid being caught. When someone is tagged, he takes over as blind man.

CAPTAINS AND CROCODILE

All the players apart from one, the 'crocodile', are blindfolded and cast in the role of Captain Hook, the pirate villain from *Peter Pan* who was scared of the crocodile that bit off his arm when he was holding an alarm clock. Ideally, the crocodile should have a loud-ticking alarm clock tied to his leg, but if you don't have one, he can simply shout 'Tick! Tock!' as he crawls around the floor on his stomach, trying to bite one of the Captains by grabbing him round the ankles. When a Captain is caught he leaves the game. The last unbitten Hook becomes the crocodile for the second round.

ARE YOU THERE MORIARTY?

Two blindfolded players, both wearing hats and armed with loosely rolled-up newspapers, sit facing each other on the floor. The first player shouts, 'Are you there Moriarty?', to which the second player must answer 'Yes!' The first player then hits out with the newspaper (not too hard), hoping to knock his opponent's hat off. If he misses, the second player asks 'Are you there Moriarty?' and when he hears 'Yes!' takes aim and strikes out. When a player manages to hit his opponent's hat off, he stays blindfolded, and the loser gives his newspaper, hat and blindfold to another player.

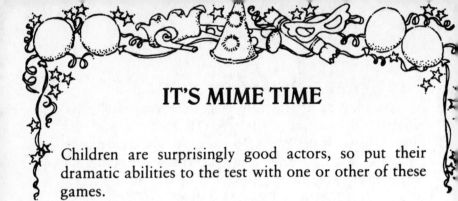

IT'S MIME TIME

Children are surprisingly good actors, so put their dramatic abilities to the test with one or other of these games.

WHAT'S MY LINE?

Jot down different occupations on separate pieces of paper and put them into a hat. The first player draws from the heat and has to mime the occupation written on the paper – dancer, jockey, sweep, painter or whatever. The person who guesses correctly draws and mimes for the next round.

GIVE US A CLUE

Put lots of book, film, play and song titles into a hat. The first player mimes whatever is on the paper he takes and the rest of his team has to guess the title. It may sound simple, but anyone who has ever tried to mime *Ninja Turtle* will know just how difficult this game can be!

Plays are indicated by the mimer taking a silent bow; films by holding a pretend camera at eye level and making a winding motion at the side; songs by a wordless impersonation of a singer; and books by clasping hands in front and opening them slowly. The number of words in the title is conveyed by holding up one finger for each, and the number of syllables in each word by holding the required number of fingers on one hand on the elbow of the other arm.

To mime 'the', make a small 't'-shape with the index finger of the right hand held vertically above the index finger of the left. 'A' or 'an' are indicated by holding the thumb and forefinger of either hand a tiny distance from each other.

Give each player a minute to get the message across to the team. If they don't get it, the other side are given a guess.

If an actor can't think of a suitable mime, he can waggle his ear. This tells his team that he's going to mime something that *sounds* like the required word or syllable.

ADVERBIALLY SPEAKING

One player goes out of the room while the others decide on an adverb – quietly, quickly, romantically, and such like. When the one who is not in the secret returns to the room he asks everyone in turn to do something in the manner of the adverb – kiss the person next to them, pick up the 'phone, turn on the television. . . If, after everyone has performed, he hasn't guessed the word, he goes out again and another adverb is chosen. But if he gets it, whoever was acting out the adverb when he guessed it has to leave the room for the next round.

WHAT ON EARTH ARE YOU DOING?

Jot down an assortment of idiotic things to do on slips of paper and put them into a hat. Things like bathing a baby giraffe, or taking a snake for a walk, holding up a sweet shop – that sort of thing. Players take it in turn to mime whatever is on the paper they draw for the others to guess. First to do so, takes the next piece of paper from the hat.

SHADOW PLAY

Pin a large white sheet across the room and weigh it down along the bottom to keep it perfectly tight. Put a lamp behind it. When the light is switched on, the sheet looks like a cinema screen. Form two teams and give each of them a selection of nursery rhyme titles, or those of films or television programmes. Team members take it in turn to go behind the screen to mime one of their titles for the other side to guess by watching the shadows cast by the light onto the screen. Suppose 'Miss Muffet' was being mimed. One of the players, Miss Muffet, could sit on the back of another player, who is crouched down on all-fours, and eat a make-believe bowl of curds and whey. When the spider scurries into view, Miss Muffet jumps up, does a silent scream and runs off.

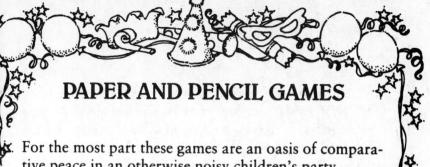

PAPER AND PENCIL GAMES

For the most part these games are an oasis of comparative peace in an otherwise noisy children's party.

AMBIDEXTERITY

Write the names of as many everyday objects as there are guests on separate bits of paper and put them into a hat. The first player takes a slip of paper from the hat and has to draw whatever is written on it *with the wrong hand*. Whoever guesses what is being drawn first, draws next.

WHAT'S WHERE?

Write out the numbers 1 to 31 on separate bits of paper and use Sellotape to stick them on various things around the house – a lamp, a table, a central heating radiator ... Now give each guest a sheet with a grid marked on it showing thirty-one numbered spaces. Players then roam about the house, searching for all the numbered objects. The first guest to fill in the sheet completely, writing down where they found each number, wins.

WHO ON EARTH?

This is an anagram puzzle game for older children. Before the party work out some anagrams of famous people's names, print them on a sheet of paper and hang it on the wall. Whoever solves the most anagrams within five minutes wins the game. Here are a few examples to give you a start:

Doll Hadar – Roald Dahl
Norman Habjour – John Barrowman
Rick Breny – Nick Berry
Danny Race – Andy Crane
Ron Pambiss – Bart Simpson
Ken Rickshaw – Nick Kershaw

BOXES

Split everyone into teams of three or four. Give each team a piece of paper and pencils. Get someone in each team to mark the paper with a grid of lines of dots, which when joined together with straight lines will make squares. Players take it in turn to connect any two dots horizontally or vertically – not diagonally. When a player completes a box, he claims it by putting his initials in it and then goes again. Whichever player has most boxes at the end of the game is the winner in that team. He or she plays the winner of another team, building up to a grand final.

MATCH THE PAIRS

The host reads out the name of one of a famous couple, fact or fiction, alive or dead. Players have to write down the names of their partners. The one who writes down the most wins. In the event of a dead heat, have a sudden death play-off by calling out a more difficult one. The first to answer is the outright winner. Here are a few examples:

Cain (and Abel)
Jack (and Jill)
Sooty (and Sweep)
Mortimer (and Arabel)
Pinky (and Perky)
Mork (and Mindy)
Tweedledum (and Tweedledee)
Bill (and Ben)

SPOT THE DETAILS

Pass two or three copies of the same picture among the players giving everyone a minute to study it before giving it to someone else. When everyone's seen it, hide the copies and ask everyone twenty questions about it. What colour were the flowers? How many people were in it? – and so on. Whoever answers most wins.

HANGMAN

Arrange guests into small teams with paper and pencils. One player from each group thinks of a famous person, or a book title, an historical event, or a film. He jots down a dash for each letter and marks off the words. Suppose he's thought of the battle of Britain. 'It's an historical event,' he'll say, and mark the paper like this:

.../ ....../../ ....

The others take it in turn to call out letters of the alphabet. If the letters they choose are included in the title, the 'executioner' fills them in in the appropriate place. If not, he starts to build the gallows, one piece being marked down for every wrong letter, followed by the condemned man's body. Players are saved if they guess the title before the executioner has completed the gallows and hanged them. The game will go something like this:

Executioner: 'It's an historical event.'
Player: 'A!'

Correct, so the executioner fills in the letters:

.../ .A..../../ ....A..
Player: 'U!'
Executioner: 'No!', and in goes the base of the gallows.

There are four parts to the gallows – the base, the upright, the crossbar and the rope – and six parts to the condemned man's body – his head, trunk, two arms and two legs.

SOUNDS AROUND

Before the party the host pre-records some everyday sounds on a cassette – a running tap, someone eating an apple, blowing his nose, ripping paper – about twenty sounds altogether. Whoever identifies most is the winner.

DOUBLE MEANINGS

Give everyone a list of clues that can be answered with two words that sound the same but are spelt differently. For younger children the clues should be straightforward: for example, the animal on top of your head (hare/hair). Older children can cope with more complicated ones such as, the inheritor can't breathe without it (heir/air).

TOUCHSTONE

Put a number of small articles including a stone in a large paper bag. If there are lots of guests you may need two or three bags, but make sure they contain the same things. The bag (or bags) is passed around from player to player, everone taking it in turn to put their hands in, trying to identify as many of the contents as possible then listing them on pieces of paper. Give a prize for the longest list.

A–Z

Write the letters of the alphabet down the left-hand side of sheets of paper before handing them out to everybody. One player (or the host) is caller. He shouts out twenty-six different categories, for example dogs, flowers, rivers, etc. Players think of a name within the categories and write it down opposite the letter it starts with. For example, if the caller says 'dogs' someone may write down 'boxer' alongside 'b' and another 'collie' opposite 'c'. The winner is the player with the most complete list – and if anyone succeeds in filling in all twenty-six spaces he or she certainly deserves a prize.

ORANGES AND LEMONS

Everyone knows the old rhyme 'Oranges and Lemons say the Bells of St Clements.' Give players a chance to make up their own versions based on ten local churches. The couplets don't have to rhyme exactly. After all, 'lemons' and 'St Clements' are hardly perfect matches.

If you live near St Anne's, St Luke's, St Belvedere's, St Mary's, St Giles', St Mungo's, St Michael's, St Jude's, St Mark's and St James's, your party guests' rhymes might go like this:

'How did you get here?'
  Say the bells of St Belvedere.
'I walked for miles!'
  Say the bells of St Giles.
'I came by bicycle!'
  Say the bells of St Michael.
'I jumped on a shark!'
  Say the bells of St Mark.
'I came by van!'
  Say the bells of St Anne.
'I rowed up the Thames!'
  Say the bells of St James.
'I flew like a fairy!'
  Say the bells of St Mary.
'I flew on a Jumbo!'
  Say the bells of St Mungo.
'This makes me puke!'
  Say the bells of St Luke.
'I think that's rude!'
  Say the bells of St Jude.

PAINT, POTS AND PAINTINGS

If you are happy to let children have the run of your house, announce a letter and send them off to write down as many things as they can spot starting with the chosen letter. Whoever produces the longest list wins. If you want to contain the party in one room, make sure that there are at least twenty things starting with the chosen letter. If it is 'c', for example, you could have a coat, a coathanger, a container, a cyclamen, a cardigan, a cheese dish, chalk and compact discs in your carpeted and curtained room – and there's ten for starters.

WHAT'S IN A NAME?

Write down the name of a famous pop group or star and hang it on the wall for all to see. Guests have to make as many words as possible using the letters in the name – three-letter words minimum. If you chose Apache Indian, words could be:

ache	pea	pin	din
hind	hen	chin	china
pain	heap	den	niche
panda	cheap	pinch	paid

and lots more!

A MENAGERIE OF LETTERS

Use a felt-tip pen to write down these anagrams on a large sheet of paper and pin it on to the wall:

shore	brae	tab	grite
fire fag	red bag	site root	peth lane
trote	drop ale	bad orral	galee
pin hold	tot as	a groan ok	zeamch pine
nine pugs	no ex	a ill rat go	plane toe

Players have to unravel the animals and write down the names of as many as they can. The ones above are:

horse	bear	bat	tiger
giraffe	badger	tortoise	elephant
otter	leopard	labrador	eagle
dolphin	stoat	kangaroo	chimpanzee
penguins	oxen	alligator	antelope

NAME THE NAMES

Give each player a paper with a Christian name written across the top. Make sure you leave a decent space between each letter. Players have five minutes to list as many other first names as they can think of under the appropriate letter. For example, under 'C' you could list 'Charlotte', 'Colin', Chris and 'Carole'.

A MIME OF INFORMATION

Divide everyone into pairs. Give each pair a pencil and paper. One of each couple goes up to the hostess who whispers something to them. He returns to his partner and mimes whatever was whispered. The partner has to draw what he thinks is being mimed. When (and if) the drawing is complete, the artist takes it to the hostess who whispers another subject to him. The artist becomes the mimer and the previous actor takes the pencil and paper ... Drawings are judged at the end of the game.

FLYING SQUAD

Give each guest a list of things you've hidden around the house. All they have to do is to find everything on the list and write down where it was. Make some difficult to find and put others where they are easy to spot.

THE SMALL 'i'

Give everyone a paper and pencil and tell them to write down capital 'A', small 'q', small 'e', capital 'F', small 'i' with a dot on it, capital 'H', small 's', capital 'B' small 'p'. Collect the sheets, and if anyone has done exactly what you've said they deserve a prize, for most people write down a small 'i' which already has a dot on it and don't think of putting another dot above it.

BLIND ART

Divide everyone into pairs and seat each couple back-to-back. Blindfold one of each pair and give the other paper and pencil. The blindfolded player is given an everyday household object – an egg whisk, iron or something of the sort – which he describes to his partner, who does his best to draw according to the description. When the artist has finished he is blindfolded and his partner takes the paper and pencil. Reward whoever has drawn most accurately what has been described.

DOUBLE PROVERBS

Give each team one slip of paper per player. On each slip is written two jumbled-up proverbs. The first team to present the hostess with a complete list of correct proverbs wins.

ONCE UPON A TIME

There should be ten bits of paper for each player. Each one has a noun written on it. Everyone takes it in turn to draw one slip at a time from the hat until everyone has their ten. They now have three minutes to write a story that somehow brings in all their nouns. The best story-teller wins.

CROSS (OUT)WORDS

Give everyone a pencil and a page of newspaper. Ideally, the same page should be photocopied once for each player, and the referee should hold a master copy of each. Players simply delete every 'the', 'of' and 'to'. After five minutes everyone hands their page to the next person in the circle for checking. The referee reads from the master page. Players gain a point for each word correctly deleted and lose one for each 'the', 'of' and 'to' they miss.

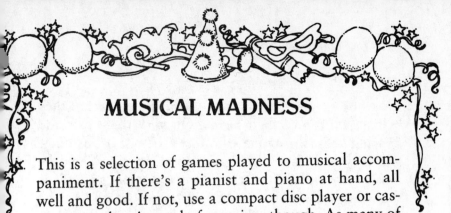

MUSICAL MADNESS

This is a selection of games played to musical accompaniment. If there's a pianist and piano at hand, all well and good. If not, use a compact disc player or cassette recorder. A word of warning, though. As many of these games involve stopping and starting the music, do this with the volume control. If you continually stop and start a tape you weaken it and it may well snap in two or you may damage your CD player.

THE CONGA

Not a game in the true sense of the word, but everyone loves forming a long line, with their hands on the hips of the person in front, and dancing along to 'Everybody Conga! Come and do the Conga! Everybody Conga! La-la-la-la-la.' Dance all over the house – upstairs, downstairs, in the garden or along the pavement! By the way, the longest-ever line of conga dancers was formed in 1988, when 119,966 people congaed the night away.

MUSICAL STATUES

This is just like 'Quite Potty' (see page 70), but played without the pots. When the music's playing everyone dances, but when it stops they must stay stock-still until it starts again. Anyone who makes a move is out, and when the music stops next time they can try to make the 'statues' move without actually touching them.

POSING AROUND

The same rules apply for this game. The only difference is that before it starts everyone draws a card on which is written an occupation – ballet-dancer, jockey, tennis-player, lumberjack ... When the music stops, everyone has to assume a suitable pose.

QUITE POTTY

Everyone is given an empty yoghurt pot which they balance on top of their heads. On with the music and dancing begins. Anyone who loses the pot drops out – and they can't use their hands to steady it. When the music stops, it's 'statue' time. Everyone stands as still as they can, while those who have dropped out try to make them shake with laughter by pulling faces or telling jokes. Anyone who moves is out of the game. More music – more dropped pots – and statues again when the music stops. The winner is the last person to keep his pot.

MUSICAL CHAIRS

One of the oldest and still one of the most popular of all games. Put a line of chairs down the middle of the room, side-by-side, with alternate chairs facing in the opposite direction. When the music plays everyone walks around the line in a clockwise direction. When it stops, they have to find a vacant chair to sit on. Going back is not allowed. If someone has just passed an empty chair he has to run right round to get to it. For the first round, have a chair for everyone. When the music is playing for the second round, remove one chair so that someone has to drop out when the music stops. The game goes on until there are two players and just one chair, but before this, when chairs are getting scarce, stand an adult or a player who is 'out' at either end of the room, and make the remaining players run around them.

MUSICAL CAPS

Seat everyone in a circle and give them all, bar one, a paper hat. When the music is playing the hats are passed from head to head. When it stops, whoever is left hatless leaves the circle and one hat is withdrawn. When there are only two players left and the music stops for the last time, the one wearing the hat wins.

PAUL JONES

Girls form an outward–facing circle inside a ring of inward-facing boys. When the music begins the circles move round in opposite directions. When it stops, everyone has to dance with whoever is facing them. 'Paul Jones' ensures that there are no shrinking violets or sad wallflowers clinging to the wall when everyone else is dancing.

THE HOKY KOKY

Is there anyone who doesn't enjoy the 'Hoky Koky'? There's bound to be someone at the party who knows how to do it, but just in case ...

> You put your right hand in, [*to the middle of the circle*]
> Your right hand out, [*behind you*]
> Your right hand in and you shake it all about
> You do the Hoky Koky [*Wave your hands in the air and shimmy down to the floor*]
> ...And you turn around,
> That's what it's all about.
> Oh! Do the Hoky Koky!
> Oh! Do the Hoky Koky!
> Oh! Do the Hoky Koky!
> That's what it's all about.

And now you put your left hand in, your left hand out ... your right leg in, your right leg out ... ending up with your whole self in, your whole self out, your whole self in and you shake it all about.. !

BACK TO BASE

Players sit in a circle of chairs. When the music starts they run round the circle. When it stops they dash back to their own chair. Last to sit down is out. They remain seated when the music starts again. Tripping is strictly illegal and penalized by a forfeit.

A LOT OF BOTTLE

Everyone balances a ping-pong ball in the mouth of an empty milk bottle and tries to keep it there as they move in time to the music, which is speeded-up as the game goes on. Anyone who drops a ball leaves the floor, until there is one, steady-handed winner.

EVER-INCREASING CIRCLES

It's sometimes difficult to get younger children to stop playing this game! Arrange everyone into groups of three, holding hands, and get them to dance round and round in time to the music. When the host shouts 'four' the groups rearrange themselves into fours... then fives, sixes, sevens – and so on. Surplus players drop out, until the host calls 'everybody' and a huge circle is formed, dancing round and round and round.

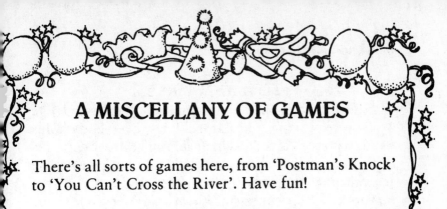

A MISCELLANY OF GAMES

There's all sorts of games here, from 'Postman's Knock' to 'You Can't Cross the River'. Have fun!

IF THE CAP FITS

Tell everyone to sit in a row – except one player who is given two hats. He puts one hat on his head and gives the other to someone else in the line. Whatever the player wearing the first hat does, the other must do the opposite. If one scratches his right nostril, the other must scratch his left; if one shakes his head, the other nods his or hers. When the second person makes a mistake he must take the first hat and give the second to a new victim.

YOU CAN'T CROSS THE RIVER

...Unless you're wearing red knickers, a blue jumper, pink socks ... One player stands on the far bank of an imaginary river, his back to the other side. He calls out 'You can't cross the river unless you're ...' and adds whatever condition he wants. Those who can cross do so: the others stay where they are. The game goes on until all but one has safely crossed. The last player on the other bank becomes the caller for the next round.

POSTMAN'S KNOCK

One of the girls is the postman (or postwoman). She leaves the room and all the boys are given a number. The postwoman knocks on the door and shouts 'I've got a letter for Number ...' The boy whose number is called leaves the room and pays for the letter with a kiss. The postwoman goes into the room and is given a number along with all the other girls. The boy who kissed her takes over as postman.

TOM AND JERRY

Choose a cat, 'Tom', and a mouse, 'Jerry', and line everyone else up in four parallel lines. Everybody holds hands with the player on either side and raises their arms to form lines of arches. On 'Go!' Tom begins to chase Jerry through the arches. When Jerry cries 'Change!' the players in the lines turn smartly in a quarter circle to the right and make new arches with the people on either side, hopefully keeping Jerry from Tom's clutches. When the cat catches the mouse, Tom becomes Jerry and a new mouser is selected.

WHISTLING IN THE DARK

One player is sent from the room and the others think up something for him to do when he is allowed to return. Kiss the tallest girl in the room; turn on the television; do a handstand – but they don't tell him what is required of him. All they do is whistle, varying the pitch according to how near he is to performing his task. It's surprising how quickly people catch on to what's expected of them!

A MONEY PUZZLE

Give everyone ten buttons. The first to arrange them in five straight lines with four buttons in each gets a prize. Here's how it's done:

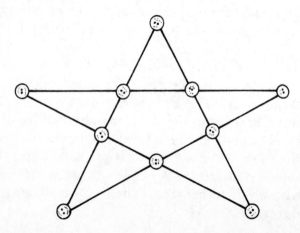

AND ANOTHER ONE

Put a strip of paper between two tumblers and balance a coin on the edge of each glass, on top of the paper. The challenge is to remove the strip of paper without dislodging the coins!

Here's how it's done: lick your right index finger and strike the paper dead centre at the top. The paper will end up between the two glasses leaving the coins on the edge.

KIM'S GAME

How observant are your guests? Put twenty small items on a tray and cover them with a towel. When everyone has gathered round the tray, remove the towel for twenty-five seconds. Replace it, then give the guests two minutes to write down as many objects as they can remember. A bonus point to those who include the tray!

GRANDMOTHER'S FOOTSTEPS

The one chosen to be 'Granny' stands facing the wall. All the others line up at the far end of the room, waiting for the word 'Go!' They then tiptoe inch by inch across the room, trying to be first to tap Granny on the shoulder. But Granny can turn around whenever she wants, and if she sees anyone moving by as much as a whisker, that person has to return to base. The first player to get close enough to touch Granny takes her place in the next round.

FOR THE EAGLE-EYED

The host tells everyone to watch him carefully and then asks one guest to do something exactly as he did it. He picks up a knife and puts it on the floor again. The chosen person does the same.

'Wrong! You're not watching properly,' says the host. He picks up the knife again the replaces it on the floor, and does it again, and again.

At last someone twigs and does exactly what the host has done ... For before picking up the knife, he has scratched his ear, or tapped the end of his nose, or something so ordinary that it is seldom spotted. The game continues until everyone has seen the light.

SNIP!

Put a 50p piece on top of a paper doily – one of the perforated kind – and balance it across the rim of a glass. Give the first player a pair of scissors and tell him to snip two of the perforations to make one larger one. Once he's done this, he passes the scissors to the next player, and everyone takes it in turn to cut away at the doily. As the game goes on all the holes in the doily gradually merge together until the coin plops into the glass. Whoever made the last cut drops out for the next round.

THUMBS UP

Players sit in the positions they are in for 'Ring the Bell' (see page 79), and when the leader gives everyone the thumbs up sign, they have to stand up as quietly as they can. When they're given the thumbs down, they sit on the floor. After four or five ups and downs the leader asks the blind man if the players are standing or sitting. If he guesses correctly, someone else is blindfolded and takes his place. If he's wrong, the game carries on where it left off. Of course, the leader can hold his thumb sideways, a signal for everyone to shuffle around quietly but to stay in the same positions.

CRAMMER

How many objects can you squeeze into a matchbox and still be able to close it easily? Put an assortment of suitable objects on the table – pins, safety-clips, matches, uncooked macaroni, needles – anything small and lots of them. Give everyone a matchbox of the same size and five minutes to cram it full (but not over-full), of the things on the table. Whoever squeezes in most wins.

PICTURE CONSEQUENCES

Children who drop out of early rounds of competitive games may well become bored watching. So it's a good idea to let them play something else that lasts until the finals of the other game, when they can cheer on their favourites. 'Picture Consequences' is ideal. Give each player a piece of paper and a pencil and ask them to draw a head and shoulders. Fold the paper down and pass it to the next player, who has to add a body, without seeing what's gone before. When the bodies have all been drawn in, the players fold the papers again and pass them round to the next ones, who fills in legs and feet. The results are usually quite comical. For example, you might get policemen's heads on ballet-dancers' bodies with rugby players' legs and boots!

BABY-FACE RACE

Divide everyone into mixed couples at one end of the room, facing a box at the other end – one box per couple. On 'Go!' the girls run to their box and pull out the top two objects, a nappy and a safety pin. (If you don't have nappies, old towels are just as good.) They dash back to their protesting partners and pin on their nappies. Then it's back to the box for the next object – a bonnet. When that's on the baby's head, it's time for the bib. Last of all, dinner. Fruit-flavoured yoghurts are ideal. Spoonful by spoonful the babies are fed and the first girl to present her clothed and fed baby to the hostess wins.

RING THE BELL

A blindfolded player with a handbell, or anything else that makes a noise, placed just in front of him, sits opposite the others who should be at the far end of the room. There's a leader standing behind the blind man. As soon as the leader points to a player, he or she begins to creep forwards as quietly as possible, hoping to get to the bell to ring it before the blind man shouts 'Stop!' and points directly at him. When a player is pointed at he returns to base and the leader indicates a new bell-ringer. The first player to ring the bell before he's pointed to by the blind man takes over as keeper of the bell for the next round.

FRENCH CRICKET

You can play this indoors, but it's much better in the garden. The player in the middle is given a tennis racquet or cricket bat. The others stand in a circle around him and try to hit his legs with a *soft* ball. The batsman uses the racquet or bat to defend himself. When he's hit on the legs, the player who threw the ball takes over in the middle. The batsman can't move his feet, and the bowlers can throw the ball between themselves before one of them 'shoots'. Batsmen score runs by passing the racquet around their bodies – one run for each round. They can also be caught out. The catcher takes over as batsman.

THE LEANING TOWER OF PISA

Stand everyone with their feet firmly together in four or five lines, everyone about a metre (1 yd) away from those around them. When the caller shouts 'To the front', players lean forwards as far as they can. The first player to stumble loses a life. The next command is 'To the back' and everyone leans as far back as possible. Then it's 'To the right!' followed by 'To the left!' Players are out when they lose their three lives.

BOTTICELLI

Players take it in turn to think of a famous person, alive or dead, real or imaginary. The others have to guess who it is. They can't ask *direct* questions such as 'Are you alive or dead?' or 'Are you fact or fiction?' until Botticelli answers 'No!' to one of the indirect questions asked. Suppose the player to go chooses Botticelli as his mystery subject. He tells the others that his name starts with a 'B'. The others ask him indirect questions to which they know the answer: 'Are you a famous composer?', for example. The questioner is thinking of Bach. If Botticelli guesses who the questioner has in mind (or another composer whose name begins with 'B'), he says 'No! I'm not Bach!' He could of course say Brahms or Beethoven instead. But if he can't think of a suitable composer, whoever ask the question has a chance to ask a direct question that establishes a fact about Botticelli – whether he is alive or dead, European or American, real or imaginary etc. If after twenty direct questions Botticelli's identity remains a mystery, he wins and selects another identity for himself. If his identity is guessed correctly, whoever got it right becomes the next Botticelli.

> *Player 1:* 'Are you a famous composer?' [*an indirect question*]
> *Botticelli:* 'No, I'm not Bach!'
> *Player 2:* 'Are you a famous pop star?' [*another indirect question*]

Now, if Botticelli can't think of a pop star starting with 'B', player 2 asks his direct question:

> *Player 2:* 'Are you alive or dead?'
> *Botticelli:* 'Dead!'
> *Player 3:* 'Are you a famous painter . . ?'

It's a game for older children, but it's a good one!

CUT THE CARDS

One corner of the room is 'Clubs', another is 'Diamonds', the third 'Hearts' and the fourth 'Spades'. Everyone dances and when the music stops everyone dashes to whichever corner they want and stays there as the host cuts a pack of cards. Players standing in whichever suit is cut are disqualified. They can join in the dancing, but when the music stops they stay where they are as the others make for the corners. When there are four players left, they must each stand in a different corner. The winner is the last player left.

CHAIN TAG

When 'it' tags another player, he holds hands with her, and the two 'its' try to tag a third player, then a fourth, then a fifth – and so on. Only the back and front players of the chain can tag, because it's against the rules of the game for players to let go of each other's hands until the last player has been tagged. He or she starts off the next round.

SMARTIE ALEX

Fill a large glass jar with Smarties (or any other sweet that's on special offer at the supermarket). Put it where everyone can see it. Guests simply have to guess how many sweets are in the jar. Whoever guesses nearest wins. The prize is the jar, and the winner has to share its contents with everyone else. Health-conscious parents may prefer to use nuts.

FLOAT THE FEATHER

Sit everyone as close together as possible on the floor. Float a feather above them. (If you can't find a feather, a scrap of tissue paper will do.) Players must stop the feather landing on them simply by blowing to keep it in the air. Players lose a life when the feather touches them. Three lives lost and they leave the game.

GONE FISHING

Cut one 'fish' per player out of old newspaper. Thread long pieces of cotton through them. Players tie the thread round their waists so that the fishes are trailing on the floor behind them. On 'Go!' fishermen try to catch each other's fish by stamping on them and pulling them off the lines. At the same time they do whatever they can to keep their own fish intact. Whoever is last to have his or her fish on the line wins.

MURDER

Put a piece of paper, once for each player, into a hat. All the papers are blank except for one, which is marked with a cross. Whoever draws it from the hat is the murderer. He kills his victims by winking at them. When a player sees he is being attacked, he falls to the floor as dramatically as possible. Players try to spot the murderer before they are killed. The game goes on until the assassin has killed everyone, or until some sharp-eyed sleuth succeeds in unmasking him!

PELMANISM

This is a memory game played with packs of cards. Make teams of three or four girls and three or four boys. Play girls against boys. The cards are put face down on the floor. The first to go in each team turns over two cards. If they are the same value – two kings, two threes or whatever – they make a trick and the player puts them on his team's side before turning over another two. If they don't match they're put back face-down in the same position. The first player in the other team now takes their turn. The secret of success in 'Pelmanism' is to concentrate very hard to remember the exact position of cards which have been turned over and replaced. The team with most tricks wins. Play it as a knock-out competition with winning teams playing each other, building up to a grand final.

THE MINUTE GAME

For this game you need someone who wears a watch with a second hand. Everyone has to sit on the floor, keep absolutely quiet and listen to some music. When the man with the watch says 'Go!', no one must move or speak until they judge a minute has passed. Then they can get to their feet. Anyone who stands up either ten seconds before the second hand has gone round once, or ten seconds after, drops out for the next round – but they do their best to distract the others from their silent count to sixty.

KING WILLIAM

One team stands at one end of the room, a second team at the other. King William stands in the middle. 'Ready! Steady! Go!' Both teams have to try to get to the opposite end without being tagged by William. If he does catch someone, he taps them on the head three times, crying 'I crown thee King' as he taps. New kings join William in the middle and try to tag the others on their subsequent sprints. Last to be crowned becomes King William for the next round.

THE 'YES' 'NO' GAME

Guests take turns at pitting their wits against the question-master, who asks questions that must be answered without using the words 'Yes' and 'No'.

'And the first contestant please. What's your
· name?'
'Emma!
'Emma?'
'That's right!'
'Emma what?'
'Emma Black!'
'Emma White?'
'No! Emma ...'
'And the next contestant please!'

HOW? WHEN? WHERE? WHY?

When one player is out of the room, the others think of a word. He returns and has to deduce what the word is by asking four questions: How do you like it?; When do you like it?; Where do you like it?; Why do you like it?

If he hasn't guessed after the four questions, he's given another round of the same questions. If he doesn't get it then, he goes out again and a new word is chosen for him. If he does guess, the next player leaves the room.

Suppose the word was breakfast:

'How do you like it?'
'Hot!'
'When do you like it?'
'In the morning!'
'Where do you like it?'
'In the kitchen!'
'Why do you like it?'
'Because everyone should go to work on it!'
'It's an egg!'

'EAR! 'EAR!

So called because players have to listen very carefully to what is being said. Two players leave the room and decide on a word. When they return to the room, they talk to each other and although they don't use the word, each sentence they use gives the others a clue. Whoever guesses the word first chooses a partner and a new secret word.

Suppose the word was 'book':

Player 1: 'I must go to the cinema and reserve seats for *Bambi*.'
Player 2: 'I haven't seen the film, but I've read it.'
Player 1: 'Did the author write lots?'
Player 2: 'Yes the library is full of them.'

''Ear 'ear' is a game for older children.

BOMBS AWAY

You have to play this game outside (unless you don't mind getting your carpet damp!), and with players who don't mind getting a wee bit wet. Blow up a few balloons and fill them with water before tying the necks. When the music's playing, players throw the balloons to each other. When it stops, anyone holding a balloon drops out. The winner is the last person in. Why do players get wet? Well, balloons do burst sometimes, don't they?

KING OF THE CASTLE

Boys enjoy playing this game. One of them, the 'King', stands on his castle – a low stool – in the middle of the floor. He challenges one of the others to try and dislodge him. If the King fights off the challenge he issues another challenge to a new claimant. A successful challenger takes the throne.

STRIPTEASE

You'll need Sellotape and lots of coloured streamers to play this game, which is much more innocent than it sounds. Cut the streamers into various lengths and stick a small piece of Sellotape at each end. Hide them all over the house so that just one end is visible. 'Ready! Steady! Go!' Off go the guests in search of the streamers. As the pieces are found, each player sticks them together one by one. The person who has the longest strip after ten minutes is the winner.

TONGUE TWISTERS

Put a selection of tongue twisters in a hat. Players take it in turn to draw one out. There's 'Sister Susie and the shirts she sews for sailors'; 'Peter Piper and his pepper', but the one that experts claim is the most difficult is 'The sixth sick sheik's sixth sheep's sick!' Anyone who can get their tongue round that deserves to get his tongue round the biggest, fruitiest ice-cream in the freezer!

THE RHYMING GAME

The first player thinks of a word but doesn't tell anyone what it is! However, he does give them a word that rhymes with it. All the others then fire questions at him. Suppose the word is 'book', the player might say that it rhymes with 'shook':

> 'Do you do it in the kitchen?'
> 'It's not cook.'
> 'Do you do it with your eyes?'
> 'No! It's not look.'
> 'Is it a chess piece?'
> 'No! It's not rook.'
> 'Is it at the end of a fishing line?'
> 'It's not hook.'
> 'Do you read it?'
> 'Yes! It's book.'

NOSEY

You'll need lots of little sachets stuffed with lavender, apples, orange peel, lemon peel – anything with a strong smell. Make the sachets by putting each item on small squares of material, bringing the corners together and securing them with cotton or an elastic band. Number each one and hang them from a line so that they're just above head height. Players take it in turn to sniff each sachet and try to guess their contents. Whoever identifies most correctly is the winner.

SHOPKEEPERS

A player leaves the room – he is 'it'. Everyone else selects what shops they're going to have – one per player. When 'it' returns he calls, 'One! Two! Three!' On three everyone calls out the name of one thing that they sell. 'It' has to guess what their shops are – baker, butcher, candlestick maker or whatever. Now someone else leaves the room. Everyone chooses another shop. The winner is the player who guesses most right.

ANIMAL, VEGETABLE OR MINERAL

One player thinks of an object. The others have to guess what it is. The only clue they're given is the answer to the first question, 'Is it animal, vegetable or mineral?' After that the only answers allowed are 'Yes' and 'No'. Whoever guesses correctly chooses the next object.

'Is it animal, vegetable or mineral?'
'Vegetable!'
'Can you eat it?'
'No!'
'Would you use it in the kitchen?'
'Er...No!' [The hesitation implies that you could use it in the kitchen, but it would be unusual.]
'Do you wear it?'
'No!'

And so on up to twenty questions or after five minutes – or until the object is guessed.

THE TASTE GAME

Play this after a boisterous game: it gives everyone a chance to get their breath back. Get everyone to pair off with someone else and sit them in two circles, one of each couple in the inside circle, facing his partner in the outside one. Players in the inner circle are blindfolded and a saucer for each pair is brought into the room. Each saucer contains two bits of apple, two orange segments, some curry powder, mustard, two Smarties, two onion rings, two potato crisps, two slivers of garlic, two slices of banana, a sprinkling of salt ... all separate from each other so the various tastes don't get mixed up. The players in the outer circle pop each titbit one by one into their partner's mouth. When the blindfolded players have sampled everything, they take the blindfold off, give it to their partners and begin to feed them. The winning couple is the one that identifies most morsels.

THREE-WAY PULL

Find a piece of rope about three metres (10 ft) long and tie the ends together. Select three players to hold the rope. Put a book on the floor behind each one. 'On your marks! Get set! Pull!' The three pull hard against each other, trying to get close enough to their book to pick it up. Winners play winners until you have a champion.

THE MAD DOG

One of the players is the 'mad dog'. Everyone else tries to avoid being tagged by him. If they are, the dog passes on his madness and is himself cured. What makes this different from an ordinary game of tag is that the dogs have to chase their prey while holding on to wherever they were bitten. So, a dog that was touched on the ankle has to hold on to his ankle while trying to catch someone else.

ON WITH THE MASK

Make a basic mask shape for each guest before the party. Put them on a table along with lots of coloured felt-tip pens, bottles of gum, feathers, streamers, glitter, Sellotape – and anything else you think may be useful for everyone to decorate their own mask. Allow ten minutes and give two prizes, one for the prettiest and one for the most frightening.

THE MARSHMALLOW MUNCH RACE

Thread a marshmallow for each player onto it's own long piece of cotton. Lay them on the floor with the free end just in front of each player. On 'Go!' they get down on hands and knees, bite at the cotton until it's in their mouths, and crawl towards the sweet, drawing the thread into their mouths as they go. Using hands is not allowed. Whoever gets to the marshmallow first is the winner. Tell players to take the cotton out of their mouths before eating the marshmallow!

SPANS

Put a large button – the 'jack' – on the floor about half a metre (20 in) from one of the walls. Give everyone a different coloured button. They take it in turn to throw their buttons at the jack from the wall opposite. After everyone has had one throw, an adult measures the distance between the jack and the buttons. A button that's landed within one handspan of the jack gains whoever threw it one point; within two spans and it's two points ... The player with the fewest points after ten rounds is the champion.

MIND READING

Before the game starts the host approaches one player and whispers a secret in his ear. He leaves the room while the host and the others choose a town or city. When he returns the host says, 'Is it. . .?'

'No!' says the 'mind reader', and keeps on saying 'No!' until the host asks, 'Is it. . .?, finally naming the chosen place.

'Yes!' is the reply. And everyone is astonished.

Naturally they think it's a fluke guess, so out goes the mind reader again, waiting until a new name is chosen before coming back to repeat his amazing feat. By now, someone may have twigged, and he volunteers to go out next time. The game goes on until one by one everybody realizes how it's done.

> 'Is it Edinburgh?'
> 'No!'
> 'Is it Birkenhead?'
> 'No!'
> 'Is it London?
> 'Yes!'

> 'Is it Dover?'
> 'No!'
> 'Is it Salisbury?'

'No!'
'Is it Liverpool?'
'No!'
'Is it Warminster?'
'Yes!'

Got it yet? The host and his partner have agreed that the town immediately before the one chosen will contain a part of the human body. It could be Ply*mouth* *Liver*pool, *Leg*horn, or even Felixs*towe*!

MIRROR ART

Anyone who has tried to draw something by following the pencil in a mirror will tell you how hard it is – but it makes a good party game. Everyone takes it in turn to sit at the table and try his hand at mirror art. Someone holds a mirror by the paper so that the artist has a clear view in the mirror of what he is drawing, but another player holds a book above the paper so that the artist can't glance down at his hand. The results usually bear little resemblance to the given subject.

ALL THE FUN OF THE FAIR

You need adults to man the stalls – because you're going to have your very own fun-fair. It takes quite a bit of pre-party planning, but it's worth it. At a real fun-fair, winners get prizes, but this is expensive, so give the adults a tally sheet each so that they can keep everyone's score. Reward the overall winner.

It adds to the atmosphere if you can find a record or tape of barrel organ music, but it's not vital.

Now then! Roll up! Roll up!

ROLL THE PENNY

Make a large grid of about 200 numbered squares – one to twenty. You'll need two or three wedge-shaped bits of wood with notches scored down the longest, uppermost side. Players roll coins down the wedges – five coins each – and score whatever number they land on. But the coin must be completely in the square: if it lands over a line, there's no score.

SPLISH SPLASH

Scatter a few one-pence pieces on the bottom of a bucket of water. Players are given three two-pence pieces each. They drop them one by one into the bucket, aiming to cover completely one of the pennies. Score one point for each penny completely covered.

MARK THE CARD

Stick some cards on a large sheet of paper, leaving a fair space between each one, and pin it on the wall. Give players five felt–tips pens each. They throw the pens tip-first at the cards, standing about two metres (6 ft) away, and score the value of each card they mark. Count ten for court cards and eleven for an ace.

STRONG MAN

Put a pair of bathroom scales in a corner, surrounded by an assortment of everyday objects – an iron, bag of potatoes, packets of sugar, books and the like. The adults weighs contestants before they pick up as much as they can carry and stand on the scales again. Subtract the body weight from the new total and award one point for each two kilograms (4 lb) of excess weight.

DUMMY RUN

An adult volunteers to run backwards and forwards across the scoring area, trying to avoid being hit by the ping-pong balls thrown by the players. One point for each strike.

CARD TOMBOLA

Put cards in old envelopes, one in each, and put the envelopes into a bag. Players take two each. If they draw a black card they add its value to their score, if they draw a red card, they subtract its value.

HUNT THE LADY

Put nine cards face up on the table – one queen amongst them. Now turn them over and move them around slowly. Players get three attempts to find the queen, with the cards being re-shuffled after each attempt. They score ten points each time they turn over the queen and lose the value of every incorrect card they pick.

HOOP-LA

Use milk bottles standing on bits of paper with a score written on each, and strong cardboard hoops. Players throw the hoops at the bottles, and if they go right over the bottle and land on the paper, they add that score to their tally.

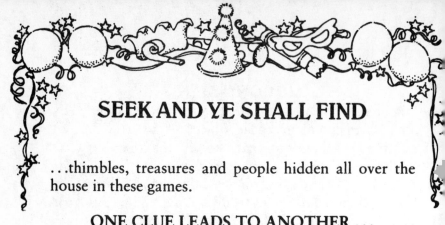

SEEK AND YE SHALL FIND

...thimbles, treasures and people hidden all over the house in these games.

ONE CLUE LEADS TO ANOTHER ...

...when you divide guests into two teams and give each one a clue that leads to another clue that leads to another, that leads to a final clue that tells the whereabouts of a treasure hidden somewhere in the house. If you hide a clue in the lavatory, the one leading to it could be 'Look here if you're desperate.' or 'Feeling flushed!' If there's a clue under the carpet in the bedroom, the clue leading to it could be 'Beneath the pile where you sleep.'

JIGSAW

Give teams half a jigsaw each – not a 5,000-piece epic view of the Tower of London, but a large-piece youngster's one. Hide the other bits around the house. The first team to find their missing pieces and complete their jigsaw wins. Anyone who finds a piece of another jigsaw as he's looking for his own is honour bound to leave it where it is. If he hides it where it is more difficult to find he gets ten forfeits.

SARDINES

One player goes off to hide and after a minute or two the others run off to look for him. Whoever finds him first squeezes in alongside him – then the next, and the next – until everyone is crammed into the same cupboard, wardrobe or whatever, apart from the last searcher. When he discovers everyone else, all trying to keep as quiet as possible (which is difficult when someone's got his elbow stuck in your ear), he becomes the sardine for the next round.

TREASURE HUNT

Tie small parcels to the ends of long pieces of wool – one for each guest – and send everyone out of the room while you hide the packages – under carpets, behind curtains, on top of the television, in the goldfish bowl – anywhere you want, and trail the wool all over the place making sure it's all well and truly entangled. Guests are given an end each and have to unravel the wool before they get to their treasure.

HIDE-AND-SEEK

Whoever is 'it' counts to 100 to give the others a chance to hide. When he's finished counting he shouts 'Coming!' and goes in search of everyone else. Last to be discovered is 'it' for the next round.

RAIL TRAIL

This is a game for older children. Scatter cryptic clues around the house. The answer to each one is the name of a British Rail station, or if you live in London, an Underground stop. The first player to find all the clues and solve them is the winner. Here are a few suggestions to start you off:

        The angry monarch (King's Cross)
        Applaud the pig here (Clapham)
        Fresh thoroughfare (New Street)
        Hose the lavatory (Waterloo)
        No one speaks to you here (Coventry)
        They man the ship (Crewe)
        The sheep's heavy (Euston)
        The fifteen-a-side school (Rugby)
        Church drink (Templemede)
        Raise the church in the air (Upminster)
        The vicar's a funny colour (Parsons Green)
        A little Alpine House (Swiss Cottage)
        Put the privet on (Edgware!)
        University town's big top (Oxford Circus)

FIT THE ADJECTIVES

Read out a short passage from a book, leaving out all the adjectives. When you get to one, say 'Blank!' When you have finished reading, give everyone a list of all the deleted words, in the wrong order. The first to list them in the right order wins.

HUNT THE THIMBLE

Make a list of ten forfeits and ten rewards, numbered one to twenty. Stuff scraps of paper also numbered one to twenty into twenty thimbles and hide them around the room. When a guest finds one of them he tells the host what number is on the paper and gets the relevant reward or forfeit. (See page 96.)

NOW IS THE TIME TO SAY GOODBYE

It's going home time. Parents are arriving to collect their children, but just before everyone leaves...

THE SECOND LAST GAME

No matter how well-planned your party is, and no matter how hard you try to make sure that everyone wins something, there are always two or three youngsters who are in danger of going home empty-handed. Have an elimination dance to ensure that the previously luckless win. Of course you have to cheat – but just a little. Blindfold the person in charge of the music and get everyone on the floor for the last dance. When he turns down the volume he tells everyone wearing red socks, ribbons, white trainers or whatever to leave the floor with their partners. Naturally he makes sure that the ones who haven't won anything so far are left on the floor at the end ... and if he has to peek over the blindfold into the mirror by the record player to do so, so what?

AND LASTLY...

Balloon bursting! What else can you do with all the balloons that are left over? Give everyone a balloon and let bedlam break out. Everyone tries to burst everybody else's balloons, using their hands only. Or, if you want to, you can tie cotton round the ends and get everyone to tie them to their legs so that the balloons are trailing on the floor behind them. Balloons are burst by stamping on them! *Never give children sharp objects to burst balloons and don't play this if there are animals in the house!*

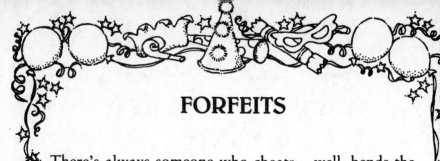

FORFEITS

There's always someone who cheats – well, bends the rules a little – maybe by using hands in a balloon race. Punishment should be swift, and what better than a quick forfeit?

Here are a few suggestions:

1 Dress up in clothes of the opposite sex and go next door to ask the time. (Warn your neighbours first!)
2 Submit to be tickled by everyone.
3 Drink a pint of very fizzy lemonade through a straw.
4 Dance to some slow ballet music.
5 Kiss everyone of the opposite sex.
6 Stand on one leg with both eyes closed for half a minute.
7 Say 'iced ink' twenty times in quick succession.
8 Eat three water biscuits – with no water to wash them down.
9 Mime to a song, karaoke-style.
10 Run the gauntlet: give everyone a lightly-folded newspaper and stand them in two lines. The guilty party has to run down the lines while being pummelled by the others.

And I'm sure you can think of lots, lots more.